# The World Economy in the 1980s: Selected Papers of C. Fred Bergsten, 1980

## Other Books by C. Fred Bergsten

*The International Economic Policy of the United States: Selected Papers of C. Fred Bergsten, 1977-1979,* 1980

*American Multinationals and American Interests* (coauthor), 1978

*Managing International Economic Interdependence: Selected Papers of C. Fred Bergsten, 1975-1976,* 1977

*The Dilemmas of the Dollar: The Economics and Politics of United States International Monetary Policy,* 1976

*World Politics and International Economics* (coeditor), 1975

*Toward a New International Economic Order: Selected Papers of C. Fred Bergsten, 1972-1974,* 1975

*Toward a New World Trade Policy: The Maidenhead Papers* (editor), 1975

*The Future of the International Economic Order: An Agenda for Research,* 1973

*Leading Issues in International Economic Policy: Essays in Honor of George N. Halm* (coeditor), 1973

*Approaches to Greater Flexibility of Exchange Rates: The Bürgenstock Papers* (coarranger), 1970

# The World Economy in the 1980s: Selected Papers of C. Fred Bergsten, 1980

**C. Fred Bergsten**
Carnegie Endowment for
International Peace

**LexingtonBooks**
D.C. Heath and Company
Lexington, Massachusetts
Toronto

**Library of Congress Cataloging in Publication Data**

Bergsten, C. Fred, 1941-
The world economy in the 1980's.

1. Economic history—1945- . 2. Economic policy. 3. International economic relations. 4. Underdeveloped areas—Economic policy. I. Title.
HC59.B484 337'.09'048 81-6031
ISBN 0-669-04658-2 AACR2



Published simultaneously in Canada

Printed in the United States of America

International Standard Book Number: 0-669-04658-2

Library of Congress Catalog Card Number: 81-6031

*To my parents*

# Contents

# Publisher's Preface

During the 1970s, a series of dramatic developments posed fundamental challenges to the international economic order: two energy shocks, pervasive double-digit inflation, the deepest recession since the Great Depression followed by widespread stagflation in most industrialized and developing nations, and unprecedented levels of capital flows with the attendant recycling problem. The system responded effectively to these challenges, for the most part, through a wide range of evolutionary steps and the adoption of basic changes, such as managed flexibility of exchange rates and negotiation of far-reaching agreements to govern the use of nontariff distortions to trade.

Nevertheless, the international economic system clearly confronts major problems at the outset of the 1980s. There is uneasiness in many quarters concerning the stability of the monetary system. Pressures are widespread to erect new barriers to international trade. Very little has been done to strengthen the framework for international investment. Tensions remain in economic relations between industrialized and developing nations.

This book includes both a retrospective appraisal of the responses to many of the international economic problems of the 1970s and a prospective analysis of the problems of the 1980s and possible responses to them. It does so through a series of presentations made in 1980 by Dr. C. Fred Bergsten, who was Assistant Secretary for International Affairs at the U.S. Treasury Department at that time (and also functioned as Under Secretary for Monetary Affairs for most of the period). The issues thus are addressed from the perspective of U.S. policy with extensive attention to the global economic system as well.

The five sections of the book cover overall U.S. international economic policy, monetary, trade, investment, and North-South developments. They encompass some of the most central economic issues of the present period: the functioning of the monetary system, recycling, the international competitive position of the United States, efforts to avoid an export-credit war, the role of the International Monetary Fund and the multilateral development banks, pursuing a "GATT (general agreement on tariffs and trade) for Investment," foreign investment in the United States, the status of North-South relations, and the growing international role of such key countries as Saudi Arabia, Brazil, and Mexico. Each chapter seeks to analyze an important aspect of international economic relations and to propose specific measures to improve them.

For many years Dr. Bergsten has been a major contributor to both the intellectual creation and practical implementation of a number of reforms of the international economic system. As Assistant Secretary (and, in 1980, de facto Under Secretary) of the Treasury, he was responsible for U.S. policy across the range of international economic issues during the four years of the Carter administration. His presentations represent both an authoritative statement of U.S. policy during that period and a thoughtful contribution to its future evolution. They represent a natural sequel to the three previous volumes of his papers published by Lexington Books, covering 1972-1974 and 1975-1976, while Dr. Bergsten was a Senior Fellow at the Brookings Institution, and 1977-1979 during his first three years at the Treasury.

# Part I
# The International Economic Policy of the United States

# 1 The International Economic Policy of the United States: An Assessment and Agenda for the Future

When President Carter assumed office in January 1977, the United States—and the world economy as a whole—confronted a wide range of difficult economic problems:

1. *Stagflation*. Both inflation and unemployment were far too high in virtually all nations. The outlook for correcting either was uncertain.

2. *Energy*. The international community had begun to finance its way out of the first oil shock but had not launched the adjustment essential to reduce energy use and increase production for the longer term. The volume of U.S. oil imports was at an all-time high. Our vulnerability was acute.

3. *Monetary Issues*. There was widespread concern over the prospects for recycling the OPEC surpluses. Some viewed Britain and Italy as ripe for financial collapse. Huge current account imbalances were developing among the industrial nations, resulting in a U.S. deficit of $14 billion and a Japanese surplus of $11 billion during 1977. As the year progressed, exchange rate instability threatened to undermine confidence in the dollar and cause international financial turmoil.

4. *Trade*. The Multilateral Trade Negotiations were stalemated by the failure of the United States and the European Community to agree on agricultural and other issues. Protectionist pressures were strong, and the new administration faced proposals for import controls in several important industries.

5. *North-South*. Relations between industrial and developing countries remained tense. Most North-South negotiations had stalemated, with major discord particularly on commodity issues.

The new administration addressed these problems in a context which was radically new for the United States. On the one hand, U.S. economic dependence upon the rest of the world had increased dramatically. Energy provides the sharpest example, but so do much broader indicators. The share of merchandise trade in U.S. gross national product (GNP) more than doubled between 1970 and 1979. The United States now depends on foreign economies to provide markets for one of every seven U.S. manufacturing jobs and 1 of every 3 acres of U.S. farmland, and international activities account for nearly $1 of every $3 of U.S. corporate profits.

---

Originally presented on December 4, 1980, before the World Affairs Council of Northern California in San Francisco, California.

On the other hand, the United States no longer dominates the course of global economic developments. United States hegemony has given way to a pluralism of industrial powers and a growing number of developing country powers, most notably in OPEC. Thus the United States confronts a kind of scissors movement—growing dependence on the world economy but declining influence, relative to other nations, to guide that economy. As a result, the maintenance of an effective international economic system is now critical to U.S. economic interests (as well as to its broad foreign policy interests, as has been the case for many years). It is within this framework that we sought to address the difficult series of international economic challenges of the past four years.

**The Overall Record**

On the whole—and recognizing the bias with which I speak—I believe that the Carter administration has compiled an outstanding record in the field of international economic policy. Before enumerating some of those successes, however, I would candidly recognize that there are key areas where our efforts fell short and much more remains to be done:

> Unacceptable levels of both inflation and unemployment remain and they remain fundamental problems for the longer term. Although our own economic recovery boosted global growth in 1977-1978 and our encouragement prodded Germany and Japan to increase their growth rates a bit later, the basic problem of stagflation has been resolved neither here nor abroad. If anything, the situation looks gloomier now than in 1977.
>
> The United States and the global community as a whole remain acutely vulnerable to further energy price hikes and supply interruptions. Adjustment has begun, but we are far from restoring even a modicum of energy independence.
>
> We have not achieved adequate congressional support for essential elements of U.S. participation in the world economy on such issues as development assistance and export expansion. Congress has approved the multilateral trade agreements, a quadrupling of our contributions to the multilateral development banks (MDBs), a seven-fold increase in the budget of Export Import Bank, and essential energy legislation—but it must do much more if the United States is to play its full role in the international economic process.

Despite these very important shortcomings, my main thesis today is that U.S. international economic policy and, more importantly, the international economic system as a whole have responded amazingly well to the unprecedented shocks of the 1970s. Virtually any observer of the international economic scene in the early 1970s, if asked to contemplate a coming decade in which unemployment rates would soar to levels unprecedented since the 1930s, inflation would reach double digits throughout the world, and two external shocks would shift global trade balances by $50-100 billion annually, would almost surely have predicted a return to trade wars and competitive exchange rate devaluation. But it did not happen. The reasons include the growing interdependence of all nations and the resultant prohibitive costs of international economic conflict, the growing habits and institutionalization of international economic cooperation, and memories of the calamitous results of such conflict in the 1930s. But our more recent reforms of the international monetary system and successful negotiations on virtually all aspects of international trade were clearly major factors in maintaining a stable, effective, and cooperative international economic system.

## International Monetary Affairs

In the monetary area, a number of key objectives have been achieved:

1. strengthening of the international monetary system and its central institutions;
2. dramatic improvement in the U.S. current account and fundamental adjustment in the payments positions of the other key industrialized countries, including disappearance of the perennial surpluses of Japan and Germany; and
3. stabilization of the dollar, and hence of the monetary system as a whole.

During this period, the international monetary system has faced unprecedented strains. Some believed that it would be unable to cope. The record shows, to the contrary, a resiliency and effectiveness unanticipated by even some of the most ardent enthusiasts of the system in the past.

First and foremost, the recycling problem has been handled effectively. Huge imbalances, totaling $50-60 billion annually after the first oil shock and over $100 billion annually now, have been channeled smoothly—mainly by the private sector—from surplus to deficit countries. There has been no financial collapse, nor will there be.

Beyond the financing, however, fundamental steps have been required for structural adjustment to this new situation, to reduce U.S. and global dependence on OPEC energy supplies. The International Monetary Fund

(IMF) (and, to a lesser but important extent, the World Bank) are playing a central and so far successful role in the global community's efforts to meet these challenges.

The Fund and Bank face complementary tasks: the Fund to encourage a judicious blend of financing and adjustment by member nations while preserving a stable international monetary system, the Bank to assist developing countries to restructure their economies and thereby to enable development to proceed as rapidly as possible in the vastly changed circumstances of the 1980s.

The IMF has forcefully demonstrated its ability to respond flexibly to changing economic conditions and members' needs. Over the past few years, with strong U.S. support, the Fund has taken wide-ranging measures to improve its ability to deal with balance-of-payments problems and promote greater monetary stability:

> Access to IMF resources has been increased sharply; members may now borrow up to 600 percent of their quotas as part of a three-year adjustment effort, six times the amount that could be obtained only a few years ago.
>
> Since present circumstances call for adjustment programs with a longer-term orientation than in the past, the Fund is now prepared to support efforts covering three years or more compared to the one-year program normally permitted earlier.
>
> Greater emphasis is being placed on supply-side considerations—in coordination with the World Bank's new structural adjustment lending program—to achieve the increases in savings, investments, import replacement, and exports required for adjustment to the new energy realities.
>
> The resources available to the IMF to help meet balance-of-payments financing needs have increased substantially as a result of expansion of basic IMF quotas in 1978 ($13 billion), the establishment in 1979 of the temporary Supplementary Financing Facility ($10 billion), and the implementation of a further $25 billion quota increase.
>
> The Fund is actively exploring the possibility of further borrowing to supplement its basic quota resources in the period ahead, including possible market borrowings.
>
> The IMF is gradually strengthening its role in the management and supervision of the operations of the international monetary system through implementation of its surveillance responsibilities.
>
> Progress is being made in developing the role of the Special Drawing Right (SDR) as a major monetary instrument, through the resumption

of allocations ($5 billion annually during 1979-1981) and improvements in the financial characteristics and usability of the SDR.

The new administration also inherited a series of major problems of balance-of-payments adjustment. There were worrisome deficits in Britain and Italy, as well as some key developing countries, which had produced loose and foolish talk of "national bankruptcies." But with key help from the IMF, Britain and Italy both adjusted successfully. Indeed, they both moved into surplus quite rapidly, and this particular problem promptly disappeared.

Much more worrisome from a systemic, as well as U.S., standpoint was the fact that the U.S. current account had deteriorated rapidly from a surplus of $18 billion in 1975 to record deficits of $14 billion in both 1977 and 1978. The deterioration was due partly to the sharp increase in our oil import bill caused by the first oil shock. It was partly a natural consequence of our own "locomotive" role in leading the recovery from the global recession of 1974-1975; our strong economic growth stimulated U.S. imports, without an equivalent increase in U.S. exports because of slow growth overseas. It also derived from the adverse effect on the U.S. competitive position of the excessive appreciation of the dollar in 1975-1976. Whatever the causes, however, the deterioration in the U.S. position raised serious concerns throughout the world and stimulated speculation against the dollar. It was clear that the deficit had to be reduced.

At the same time, the external positions of Japan and Germany yielded a combined surplus of $15 billion in 1977. In 1978, the Japanese surplus alone exceeded our own deficit. Reducing disparities in economic performance and thus these imbalances among the major countries was an immediate and central policy objective of the new administration, dating from Vice President Mondale's trip to Europe and Japan only three days after the inauguration.

Starting in late 1977, the German and Japanese economies shifted toward stronger expansion of domestic demand. Needed exchange rate changes took place. By 1979, imports in both Germany and Japan increased substantially and their current account surpluses disappeared. Indeed, both swung into sizable deficit. The adjustment process demonstrably worked, and both countries contributed enormously to stabilizing the global economic and financial system.

The United States, for its part, has eliminated its current account deficit, which many observers, as recently as two years ago, regarded as endemic. Despite an increase of over $40 billion in U.S. oil import costs since 1978, our overall current account has improved by almost $15 billion. The U.S. current account will be in balance (or better) in 1980 for the second straight year. We expect it to be in approximate balance, perhaps in modest surplus, next year as well. Indeed, today the U.S. current account is the strongest among the OECD nations. Together with the stabilizing changes in the other key industrial countries, these developments provide strong testimony that the adjustment process works.

In November 1978, the United States also moved to more active intervention in the foreign exchange market to halt an excessive depreciation of the dollar and maintain orderly conditions necessary to global confidence. In retrospect, I believe that the program of November 1978 marked a watershed in U.S. international monetary policy. For perhaps the first time, the U.S. government recognized that the relationships among domestic performance, external balances, and exchange markets are so strong that external factors must on occasion go far to determine our internal policies. From that date, there was unanimity within the administration (and the Federal Reserve) that fighting inflation had to be the priority objective of U.S. economic policy—in important part because a failure to do so would continue the vicious cycle of a weaker dollar abroad and yet more inflation at home.

As a result of these developments, the dollar has increased in value by an average of over 9 percent in terms of other major currencies over the last two years. The increases against the DM and the yen are even greater—about 14 percent and 23 percent, respectively, as of December 2. We expect continued dollar—and international monetary—stability into the foreseeable future.

**Trade**

When the Carter administration took office, trade issues stood at a critical juncture:

> The U.S. trade balance had experienced an $18 billion deterioration during the two previous years, from a $9 billion surplus in 1975 to a $9 billion deficit in 1976. The deficit widened considerably (to $31 billion) during 1977 as import growth strongly exceeded the growth of exports.
>
> Protectionist pressures in the United States were mounting, spurred by high unemployment, increased import generation in sensitive industries, and a sense that foreign industries benefited from unfair subsidies and pricing practices. Major escape clause cases were pending for shoes, television sets, and sugar, and it was widely feared that Congress would override the president if some form of import restraints was not adopted.
>
> The first court decision in the Zenith case was imminent, with potentially explosive effects on some of the most basic rules of the international trading system.

The Multilateral Trade Negotiations, initiated in 1973 to further liberalize international trade and work out new trading rules, were deadlocked, with no prospect for progress in sight.

The new administration responded decisively to these challenges, emphasizing (1) efforts to improve U.S. export performance, (2) further global trade liberalization, and international cooperation to resolve common trade problems and reduce government distortions to trade, and (3) open markets at home.

Our current competitive position provides a strong basis for the future improvement of U.S. exports. Contrary to much conventional wisdom, the United States has improved its competitive position in international markets over the past decade. On the basis of volume data (as distinct from nominal value shares in dollar terms, which distort market shares due to exchange rate fluctuations), the U.S. share of industrial nations' exports rose from a trough of 19.2 percent in 1971 to 20.8 percent in 1979 and 21.1 percent in the first half of 1980. From 1978 through the first half of 1980, in particular, the volume of U.S. nonagricultural exports has risen about twice as fast as world trade—indicating a rapid rise in our share of world export markets. This development is particularly encouraging because it is consistent across most industry categories.

For the future, however, we need to do even better—to pay for oil imports, maintain a stable dollar, and support our domestic economic objectives. Thus it is crucial to check inflation, improve U.S. productivity, reduce disincentives to exports, and increase the export consciousness of both the U.S. business community as a whole and all parts of the U.S. government, building upon the strong trend of the past three years. To contribute to this effort, the administration has increased financial support by the U.S. Export-Import Bank for U.S. exporters sevenfold, prepared a major review of government disincentives to exports, and supported legislation to stimulate the formation of export trading companies to assist small businesses in obtaining the capital and expertise necessary for developing foreign markets.

The successful conclusion of the Multilateral Trade Negotiations during 1979 achieved an overall reduction in industrial tariffs of approximately 30 percent, as well as important new codes on the use of government subsidies, standards, and procurement, and new dispute resolution procedures. The new package of agreements should help ensure that international trade is both more open and fairer for all nations, and it should further increase U.S. export opportunities. The new Subsidies Code is an especially important achievement in providing vital international discipline over the use of both domestic and export subsidies. A number of key developing countries have joined the codes, and it is hoped more will do so in the future.

The United States and other major trading nations have also negotiated an International Arrangement on Official Export Credits as a means of reducing trade distortions due to subsidized export credits. Efforts are currently under way to broaden and update this arrangement to address the remaining problems of export credit competition, whose subsidy costs are still huge. Estimates for 1979 run as high as $5 billion. The Venice Summit set a December deadline for completion of these negotiations. If they are not successful, the United States will derogate from the current agreement—primarily by extending much longer maturities on our own export credits than are permitted under the Arrangement—to meet foreign competition and assure a fair shake in international markets for U.S. exporters.

In East-West relations, the United States has achieved significant progress in normalizing economic relations with the Peoples' Republic of China, including a claims/assets agreement, a trade agreement, maritime and textile agreements, and expansion of scientific and technical exchanges. United States-China trade has virtually quadrupled from $1.2 billion in 1978 to an estimated $4 billion this year. China has also joined the IMF and the World Bank, and can be expected to participate actively in these key international institutions in the future. Notwithstanding the necessity for economic sanctions against the Soviet Union, we have continued to develop bilateral economic relations with the Eastern European nations.

To avoid mutually disruptive import protectionism, the United States has supported annual renewals of the Organization for Economic Cooperation and Development (OECD) Trade Pledge and the adoption of a new permanent Declaration on Trade by the OECD ministers, with provision for annual review and discussion of major trade problems. Domestically, we have maintained a basically open market, despite strong pressures for import restrictions. Specifically, the administration has:

Rejected across-the-board import restraints;

Negotiated temporary orderly marketing arrangements (OMAs) to slow the pace of television and shoe imports from key suppliers, but rejected more restrictive import quotas, resisted pressure for OMAs on shoes with additional suppliers, and significantly liberalized the OMAs for color televisions this year;

Adopted a trigger price mechanism for steel to improve the implementation of our antidumping statute, rather than limit the level of steel imports;

Negotiated an international arrangement on sugar with floor price provisions;

Appealed and won a reversal of the Zenith court decision that Japanese rebates of a domestic consumption tax, acceptable under the General

Agreement on Tariffs and Trade, constituted a government bounty that should be countervailed.

Resisted pressure to limit auto imports, and insisted on waiting for a decision by the U.S. International Trade Commission on whether auto imports are causing injury;

Added a number of items to the U.S. system of generalized preferences (GSP) for duty-free imports from eligible developing countries.

The administration has adopted limited import restraints only in response to injurious foreign dumping or subsidies, or as a temporary response to dramatic surges in imports which threaten U.S. industries. We have adopted comprehensive programs to address the problems of the key automobile and steel industries as they adjust to foreign competition. Continuing government-business-labor discussions should help develop mutual efforts to improve productivity and modernization of these industries for the longer term, obviating the need to respond at the border.

## Energy

When this administration came into office, the world had successfully weathered the immediate demands of financing the dramatic increase in energy prices caused by the oil shock of 1973-1974. The emphasis on financing, however, deflected attention from the longer-term issue of fundamental economic adjustment to higher levels of energy costs, which were still working their way through the global economy.

By 1977, U.S. oil imports hit record levels. There had been little U.S. adjustment in terms of energy conservation, reduced oil imports, or increased production of alternative sources of energy. The United States continued to control domestic oil prices, thereby cushioning the effect of global prices and maintaining a continuous source of relatively inexpensive energy at home—with little incentive to conserve or increase domestic production. In a similar manner, most developing nations had turned to external finance to maintain domestic energy consumption and economic growth, rather than taking initial steps toward longer-term adjustment.

The new U.S. administration therefore faced the very difficult task of convincing both Congress and the American public, as well as the international community more broadly, that such fundamental adjustment was vital. Largely as a result of the second oil shock of 1979, all nations now seem convinced of this necessity. From a slow start, the United States has now made substantial progress toward its longer-term objectives. Our energy policy has been twofold in nature: (1) to develop a strong domestic program of conservation and alternative energy production; and (2) to promote international cooperation among oil-consuming countries to reduce dependence on imported oil. A number of measures have now been adopted:

> The President implemented a program for replacement-cost pricing of domestically priced crude by phased price decontrol ending October 1, 1981. A Windfall Profit Tax was secured to reap for the nation a fair share of decontrol revenues.
>
> The Natural Gas Policy Act of 1978 will phase out price controls on new natural gas by 1985 and eliminate the artificial distinction between intra- and interstate pricing.
>
> A Synthetic Fuels Corporation has been authorized for the purpose of supplying at least 500,000 barrels per day of synthetic fuels from domestic sources by 1987 and 2 million barrels per day by 1992.
>
> A Solar Energy and Energy Conservation Bank has been implemented to assist in encouraging conservation and solar energy.

As a result of these measures, and others adopted earlier:

> Net oil imports have fallen dramatically from a peak of 8.5 million barrels per day in 1977 to 6.6 million barrels per day in the first half of 1980—a 25 percent decline—and are expected to be even lower in 1981.
>
> Oil consumption in the first half of 1980 dropped 8.5 percent below the same period in 1979 and gasoline consumption dropped by 7.7 percent.
>
> The ten most energy-intensive industries in the United States have achieved a 14 percent improvement in energy efficiency and are now saving the equivalent of 1.2 million barrels per day compared to 1972.
>
> Domestic oil reserves discovered in 1979 totalled 2.2 billion barrels, the best results since 1974.
>
> The domestic ethyl alcohol program, for use in gasohol, should result in domestic production of 500 million gallons of alcohol by the end of 1981.
>
> Coal production increased from 599 million tons in 1973 to 776 million tons in 1979. United States coal production may provide one of our best sources of both alternative energy production and increased exports to offset the cost of oil imports in the 1980s.

International cooperation is also taking shape through the International Energy Agency (IEA) and the economic summits. The May 1980 IEA ministerial agreed on a system to restrain demand in the case of a supply emergency. The seven major industrial nations agreed at the June 1979 Tokyo Summit to establish individual country import targets for 1980 and 1985; similar targets were subsequently adopted by all IEA countries. At the Venice Summit, participants agreed to take additional measures to conserve in all sectors and to achieve a collective oil savings of 15-20 million barrels per day by 1990 through the development of coal, nuclear, synthetic, and renewable energy sources.

To lessen dependence of developing countries on imported oil, the World Bank has dramatically stepped up its lending for energy development projects in oil-importing developing countries. It projects lending of $14 billion for this purpose through 1985, with estimated production increases in less developed countries (LDCs) equivalent to 2-2.5 million barrels of oil per day—and thus an important impact on the world supply/demand balance. The Bank is now exploring ways to further enhance energy development in its borrowing countries, including the possibility of creating a new energy facility or affiliate to do so.

In less than a decade, the world has undergone a truly epochal change: from an era of cheap, secure energy to an era of expensive, insecure energy. No end is yet in sight for either price escalation or supply instability. Much more clearly needs to be done. We have only just begun to make the needed adjustments to a continuing global energy problem. But the policy changes and results of the past few years suggest that a major start has been made, with promise for continued fundamental adjustment in the years ahead.

### North-South Relations

When the Carter administration took office, North-South relations had begun to emerge from the confrontations of 1973-1974 but were still tenuous at best. It was clear that comprehensive global negotiations (as represented by the experience with the Conference on International Economic Cooperation) were not the best forums for developing concrete solutions to broad economic problems.

We therefore adopted a strategy of seeking substantive progress on specific economic issues in the individual functional institutions (primarily GATT, the IMF, and the development banks) responsible for each. Our goal was to address common problems to the mutual benefit of all countries, industrialized and developing alike. We believe there has been major progress as a result—though one must recognize, at the same time, that this has proven the most difficult area in which to generate public and congressional support for our efforts.

More than $90 billion in replenishments for the multilateral development banks (MDBs) have been agreed upon since President Carter took office. The United States has supported a capital increase for the World Bank of $40 billion. We took the lead in negotiating a replenishment of almost $10 billion for the Inter-American Development Bank. We participated in negotiating a new replenishment of over $2 billion for the Asian Develpment Fund and have agreed to U.S. membership in the African Development Bank and an increase in its capital of $4.5 billion. For IDA, the concessional window of the World Bank, which is the most important concessional assistance institution in the world, we contributed 31 percent to the fifth replenishment of $7.6 billion in 1977 and pledged 27 percent to the sixth replenishment (IDA VI) of $12 billion beginning this year. United States annual appropriations to the MDBs as a whole increased from $695 million in fiscal year 1976 to $2.5 billion in fiscal year 1979.

Some of these major steps, however, such as the World Bank capital increase and IDA VI, remain to be approved by the Congress. Moreover, delays in fulfilling our international commitments, including congressional failure to act on IDA and cutbacks in the regional banks, present serious problems in carrying out these accomplishments. This can severely hamper our own security and economic interests in the developing nations, which provide the largest potential growth markets for U.S. exports in the 1980s.

On the qualitative side, the World Bank is positioning itself to provide greater assistance to encourage energy production in the developing countries, as already noted, and necessary structural changes in the economies of the developing countries. The Bank, in a significant departure from past lending practices, is now providing nonproject structural adjustment loans to member countries. These loans, coordinated closely with the IMF, can make a major contribution to the development of recipient countries in the changed context of today's world economy while also strengthening the recycling process.

Regarding commodity policy, perhaps the major source of North-South tensions in the mid-1970s, the administration reversed the practice of its immediate predecessors and has supported the negotiation of commodity stabilization agreements to reduce price volatility, lessen inflation, and stabilize resource availability:

An International Sugar Agreement was completed in 1977.

A Natural Rubber Agreement was completed last year, and has been ratified by Congress.

In early 1980, Congress authorized a U.S. contribution to the International Tin Agreement to help stabilize the world price; negotiations on a new agreement are continuing.

Consumers and producers have recently reached an agreement revising the economic provisions of the International Coffee Agreement.

> After three years of negotiations, a Common Fund Agreement was concluded in June 1980.
>
> But we will not participate in arrangements which are not economically viable. We were not members of the previous International Cocoa Agreement, and we are unlikely to join the newly negotiated ICA because its floor price is far above realistic levels.

As a result of all these steps, international commodity arrangements now contribute modestly to fighting world inflation, and commodity issues are no longer a matter of serious contention in North-South relations.

The Multilateral Trade Negotiations (MTN) have resulted in a 25 percent cut in developed country tariffs on items of traditional export interest to the developing nations. Excluding textiles and apparel, U.S. tariff cuts on LDC products average even higher, about 35 percent. The new codes will provide a more open and stable environment for future LDC trade growth, as well as a permanent legal basis for special and more favorable treatment of developing countries and more liberal rules on trade measures taken by LDCs for development purposes. Since opportunities for trade expansion are probably the single most important feature of the world economy for most developing nations, the MTN agreements marked an enormous step forward in North-South economic relations.

LDCs have also benefited from a generally open U.S. market for LDC products. Despite the fact that the United States accounts for only about 36 percent of the combined GNP of the industrial countries, in 1978 the United States took more than 52 percent of developing country manufactured exports to all industrial countries. Nearly 22 percent of all our manufactured imports in 1978 came from developing countries; the corresponding figure for all other industrial countries was less than 5 percent.

We and other donors have substantially increased concessional assistance to the poorer developing countries. Between 1970 and 1978, aid receipts by countries with per capita income under $400 tripled. Measured in relation to the GNP of the recipient countries—which is probably the best overall indicator of the contribution of aid flows to a recipient's development—total official aid to the poor countries has sharply increased over the past few years. For the least developed countries, aid receipts increased from 2.6 percent of the recipients' combined GNP in 1969-1971 to 10.3 percent in 1978. For all countries with per capital GNP below $400, the growth was from 3.3 to 4.7 percent.

Finally, the numerous measures in the monetary area which I have already summarized have special significance for the developing nations, which are so dependent upon external resources, to tide them over this difficult period. They can now borrow much more from the IMF, on longer terms, and with more balanced adjustment programs. Developing countries are clearly major beneficiaries of the monetary reform of the past few years.

**Investment**

More than ever before, investment has become an engine of future economic growth and a key factor influencing future trade flows. Increased domestic investment has become a common objective of all nations to support more jobs, more exports, more productive capacity to fight inflation, and new technologies.

Governments frequently adopt measures, however, which can distort the allocation of investment among nations, reduce the potential gains from international specialization, and prompt countermeasures by other governments. Key problems involve the use of financial, trade, tax, and other incentives to attract foreign investment which might otherwise locate elsewhere, and the imposition of performance requirements which seek to tilt the economic benefits stemming from particular investments to one country at the expense of others.

However, there is at present virtually no international regulation of government actions in the investment field—no guidelines for what is acceptable, no recognized recourse against harmful actions by others. This is anomalous in view of the huge volume of such investment and in comparison to the elaborate rules which we have developed in the trade and monetary areas. The problems resulting from government interference in this area are proliferating and will become even more troublesome in the decade ahead.

Emulation is especially visible in the auto sector. The offer of investment incentives has become a key factor in winning new auto plants in Canada, France, and the United States, among others. Brazil and Mexico require foreign companies to produce locally up to 100 percent of the value added as a condition of participation in their automobile industries—equivalent to zero import quotas which are relaxed only if the companies expand their exports.

During the past four years, the United States has begun to object strongly to the use of incentives and performance requirements, recognizing that pressures are building for the United States to impose similar requirements on foreign companies which locate here to ensure the use of U.S. parts and labor. Investment incentives and performance requirements distort basic investment decisions and subsequent trade flows. They can have the effect of shifting the location and benefits of investment across national borders, thereby exporting the problems of the country using them to others. By the time trade flows, irreversible decisions have been made, and the damage is extremely difficult to undo.

International trade mechanisms, such as the new subsidies code, provide the only existing means to address investment problems internationally—but they are not sufficient. We do not have rules of the game, or even a code, for investment incentives or performance requirements. We should. Even more basic, but more long-term in nature, we should have a "GATT for investment" similar to the GATT we now have for trade: a common body of rights and regulations which defines acceptable actions and provides recourse for those whose rights are harmed.

Improved international cooperation has become a key objective of this administration in the investment area, and we have made some progress:

> The OECD is studying the effect of investment incentives and disincentives on the international investment process and international economic relations.
>
> An Investment Task Force (which I chaired) under the auspices of the IMF/World Bank Development Committee, has endorsed the objectives of (1) seeking an international understanding which would limit the adverse effects of investment incentives and (2) considering what further actions might need to be taken with regard to performance requirements. It also laid out in some detail what an arrangement to limit incentives could look like.

Continuing efforts will be needed in multilateral and bilateral fora to assure that these beginnings bear fruit over time. This will undoubtedly be a central area for international negotiations in the future.

## A Look Ahead

In sum, much has been accomplished. The United States has balanced its current account and stabilized the dollar. The international adjustment process has worked effectively. The international monetary and trading systems have met unprecedented challenges and been strengthened for the future. Energy programs are developing which will reduce our dependence on volatile oil supplies. North-South relations have improved substantially.

At the same time, as already indicated, many important international economic problems have not yet been resolved. Moreover, new issues are arising with disconcerting rapidity. The agenda for the future remains full, and I will indicate some of its specifics in a moment.

Beneath the specifics, however, lie three fundamental questions. The first derives from the eternal verity—often forgotten—that our international economic policy begins at home. The strength of our domestic economy, and the effectiveness of our "domestic" economic policies, have a profound effect on our success in achieving U.S. international economic objectives. High rates of unemployment and a stagnant economy at home not only weaken the entire world economy, they generate strong pressures to restrict imports and reduce domestic support for foreign assistance programs. Inflation in the United States transmits inflationary pressures to the rest of the world, weakens our competitive position, and creates doubts about the soundness of our currency—the world's key currency.

The first key question facing U.S. international economic policy in the years ahead is thus whether we can get our own house in better order. The achievements of U.S. international economic policy over the past few years are particularly remarkable, in fact, in light of the unsettled state of our economy. For the future, however, it is essential that the United States reduce both inflation and unemployment substantially and resume rapid productivity growth. Success in doing so will go far to determine the ability of our nation to resist protectionism and play its full role in international economic cooperation, as well as maintain the strength of U.S. exports and the dollar.

The second question presents what I believe will be the central strategic issue for U.S. international economic policy in the 1980s. Traditionally, the United States has done abroad what it does at home. This is true for the whole range of our interactions with the rest of the world: taxation, antitrust, export finance, morality issues such as human rights and "corrupt business practices" to name just a few.

The problem is that virtually every other country has based its international economic policy on an opposite premise. They do abroad what everyone else (excluding the United States) does abroad—on the view that such behavior is essential to compete effectively. The United States and the rest of the world simply operate on very different—indeed, opposite—basic philosophies.

From the U.S. standpoint, such a conflict was of marginal importance as long as the international component of our economy was very small or our dominant economic position assured a strong U.S. influence on others' policies. Today neither condition holds.

The United States must therefore seriously ask whether it can continue to apply a single standard for behavior both at home and abroad—or whether a different standard is necessary in the international arena, where we cannot unilaterally control the activities of other nations and may need to match them on their own terms in order to remain competitive. Should we continue to prohibit U.S. firms from activities in the international market which have no impact on competition at home—or even those which do—if the gains abroad outweigh the costs at home? Should we let banks invest in export trading companies as a means of expanding U.S. exports, even though we will not let them take part in such commercial activities at home? Should we continue to hamper U.S. trade on morality grounds such as "corrupt business practices," boycotts, and human rights? Should we do so in order to preserve tax equity between Americans working abroad and those working at home? Should we insist on financing our exports at U.S. interest rates rather than those derived in the global competitive market place?

A closely related question is whether we should fight or join the trend toward government intervention by other nations, who increasingly use the tools of domestic and international economic policy to tilt the benefits of trade and investment in their direction. If Europe restricts imports of Japanese automobiles, diverting further competition to our open market, should we continue to resist restrictive actions ourselves? If other nations subsidize official export credits to gain a competitive edge in world markets, or impose export performance requirements on those who would invest in their domestic markets, should we compete on their terms?

The clear preference of the United States, under administrations of both parties and in the Congress as well, has been to negotiate common rules for the international marketplace—based largely on our own standards—to assure equal competitive opportunities for all parties. But where other nations refuse to do so, we may want to counter with equivalent policies of our own. Yet we must also recognize that the implications for our domestic economy of such policy changes could be profound, and we should carefully weigh the costs as well as the potential benefits of such an approach before embarking upon it.

Each of the issues I have cited in this context is now being addressed on its own. Indeed, in some areas—such as export finance and tax policy—we are already moving toward a new philosophy, at least to a limited extent, of doing abroad what others do abroad. There are even a few historical cases of such an approach (for example, the Webb-Pomerene Act regarding export cartels). But I believe that the United States needs to confront directly the issue of whether the fundamental premise of the past will be relevant for the future—and decide its course on specific issues, such as those cited, in light of the conclusion which is reached.

The third key question asks whether we can support at home what we are doing abroad. If we cannot sell to Congress and the American public the obligations to which we have committed the United States in international negotiations, our efforts are not only fruitless but may even undercut the viability of the international economic system itself. Passage of our domestic energy legislation was essential in dealing with the global energy crisis, yet Congress could not agree on what action to take for years. Congressional reluctance to pass key authorizations for development assistance has meant that we must begin negotiations anew, and our own ability to deliver on our international commitments will be further questioned by other nations.

The need to sustain domestic support for a continued strong U.S. involvement in the world economy is the most critical item of all on the agenda for the future. The United States reaps huge benefits from the global economy in terms of jobs, markets, stimulus to efficient production, consumer choice, and GNP. We cannot expect to continue to reap these benefits—let alone increase them—without maintaining strong support at home for our efforts overseas. This will be a continuing battle for U.S. policy officials but an essential ingredient for an effective international economic policy for the 1980s.

There is a close relationship among the three issues cited. It is likely that a strong, healthy domestic economy and a more aggressive U.S. competitive stance abroad would go far to mobilize public support for a constructive U.S. international economic policy. Indeed, such developments may be prerequisites for—and integral components of—such a policy. The success of our nation in dealing with these issues will, I believe, go far to determine the nature and success of both the U.S. economy and overall U.S. foreign policy in the decade ahead.

Turning to details, the agenda for the coming years is already very full, beyond the obvious "domestic" needs already cited:

> Further major efforts are needed in the energy area, particularly in building a sizable strategic reserve here at home and achieving proven consumer cooperation to defend against disruptions in OPEC oil prices and supplies—with an ultimate objective of effective producer/consumer negotiations to assure greater stability on both sides of the market.
>
> Orderly evolution of the international monetary system is needed both to achieve greater stability in exchange markets and to accommodate the growing use of a number of national currencies in international finance, including a greater role for the IMF in guiding the system and for the SDR as the principal reserve asset.
>
> The IMF and the multilateral development banks need to have adequate resources to meet the demands of continued payments and development problems, particularly to assure continued effective international response to the recycling problem.
>
> The time has come to create a "GATT for investment": new international rules to discipline government activities in the investment field, similar to those we now have for trade and monetary relations.
>
> And defensive actions must be maintained to resist protectionist trade barriers for domestic industries and to preserve effective world economic

> management by insisting that North-South economic relations progress through functional fora rather than grand political schemes for "a new international economic order."

The international economic agenda for the 1980s is extensive and will be crucial to both the United States and the global economy. Support for a constructive U.S. international economic policy has always been bipartisan in nature. The task for the period ahead will be to assure that we keep it that way.

# Part II
# The International Monetary System

# 2 The International Monetary System in the 1980s

This chapter discusses the outlook for the international monetary system in the 1980s. The system is clearly in a period of considerable change; its satisfactory evolution in coming years will require active cooperation and management by monetary authorities. At the same time, the system we have today has weathered some very serious storms with reasonable success—a record that is frequently ignored but which provides a strong basis for confidence that the challenge will be met.

I would like to focus discussion on three subjects: the experience with balance-of-payments adjustment during the latter part of the 1970s and its implications for the future; developments in international reserves and liquidity; and the role of the International Monetary Fund (IMF) in guiding the evolution of the system on the basis of its authority in the complementary areas of adjustment and liquidity.

## The Balance-of-Payments Adjustment Process

It has become fashionable in some circles to argue that the adjustment process does not work. Some have taken the view that the shift to flexible exchange rates in 1973 not only has failed to promote adjustment but has actually hindered adjustment, created disorderly market conditions, and permitted exchange rate movements that are too large and too frequent. At the extreme, some have argued that the present arrangements constitute no system at all, because they are not formalized in the neat fashion of the Bretton Woods par value and convertibility arrangements.

These views are wrong. We do have a system. It is not perfect, but it clearly works. Indeed, the adjustments which occurred in the latter 1970s rank among the major success stories of the period—or of any period of international economic adjustment.

In 1974, the world financial system sustained the worst shocks and disruptions of the postwar period. The global pattern of current account imbalances was abruptly altered by massive transfers of purchasing power to oil producers, a sharp acceleration of inflation rates, and a plunge of the world economy into recession. The OPEC current account surplus rose

---

Originally presented on October 28, 1980, before the Center for International Business in Dallas, Texas.

from virtually zero to about $70 billion. The current account position of the oil-importing countries deteriorated correspondingly, with a particularly pronounced shift in the position of the industrial countries from moderate surplus to large deficit.

Patterns of imbalances within the industrial country group led to serious strains on the international financial system. Many observers believed that Italy and the United Kingdom were on the verge of national bankruptcy by the end of 1974. Loose (and foolish) talk suggested that these countries had lost all ability to influence their economic destiny.

Fortunately, this was not the case. By 1977, the Italian current account was again in surplus, and the British deficit had been virtually eliminated. These changes in part reflected cyclical and energy developments. But the most important part of the story was that both countries pursued demand management policies that encouraged export production and reduced dependence on imports and permitted exchange rate adjustments to compensate for relatively high domestic inflation.

The more recent evolution of current account balances among the United States, Japan, and Germany provides similarly strong evidence of successful adjustment. Barely two years ago, it was widely believed that Japan and Germany were in permanent surplus and that the United States was in permanent deficit. Stories about an irreversible decline in the U.S. competitive position abounded.

Again, such views have proved to be wrong. In 1980, the U.S. current account is likely to be in balance for the second straight year. Despite a rise of over $40 billion in our oil imports since 1978, our overall current account has improved by about $15 billion and is now the strongest in the Organization for Economic Cooperation and Development (OECD) area. We are likely to run at least a modest surplus in 1981. Our export volume has been rising twice as fast as world trade for two and one-half years. On the other side of the equation, Japan and Germany have moved into substantial deficit in 1979 and 1980 and seem likely to remain there at least through 1981.

Again, the changes have been partly cyclical and energy related. But they also reflect coordinated efforts by the countries concerned to correct their positions through appropriate domestic economic policies, and the effects of exchange rate changes.

The overall effect has been a much more sustainable pattern of imbalances throughout the OECD area and the restoration of general exchange market stability. On a trade-weighted basis, the dollar is about 6 percent above its lowest level of two years ago. The record contrasts sharply with the fears of grave monetary disruption, even collapse, that were expressed even quite recently by some observers.

Hence the adjustment process, as traditionally defined, has worked effectively. It augurs well for the future of the international monetary system.

It suggests that our international mechanisms, institutions, and methods of cooperation have registered impressive success in fulfilling their tasks.

At the same time, this success story has been overshadowed by the continued dependence of the world on imported oil. After the first oil shock, the major industrial countries and most of the developing nations were able to correct their short-term positions. This was possible in large part because of the fall in the real price of oil in 1975-1978.

But the world did not adjust sufficiently to the fundamental shift in the energy situation which had begun to take place. After demand for oil was reduced temporarily by recession, the oil-importing world to a large extent financed continuing high levels of consumption and failed to put in place the new investments required to reduce its dependence on imported oil. A second round of massive oil price increases, beginning in early 1979, thus has brought a renewal of huge imbalances between OPEC and the oil-importing world—compounding the problems of a world economy still beset by strong underlying inflationary pressures and laboring under heavy external debt burdens accumulated during the last decade.

This second oil shock has also brought, finally, clear realization that repeated oil shocks cannot be avoided without deliberate adjustment to a radically altered world economic and energy balance. The required adjustments involve both energy conservation and development of new energy sources. They must encompass measures to stimulate investment and productivity in circumstances of greatly increased energy costs.

Significant progress is at last being recorded in all these areas. For the industrial countries as a group, the volume of oil imports was lower in the first half of this year than at any time since 1973. In volume terms, oil imports in the first half of 1980 were 14 percent lower than the peak level of 1977. The U.S. improvement weighs heavily in these aggregate gains. United States oil imports so far this year are about 25 percent below the peak rate of 1977, and oil consumption is trending down. Some of this, of course, is attributable to reduced economic activity. But it is primarily the result of improved energy efficiency. The ratio of energy use to economic output in the United States is now about 10 percent below the ratio in 1973. Further progress is essential, but the trend is clear and strong.

As a whole, the non-oil-developing countries have not adjusted as rapidly as the industrial countries in response to the new economic environment. During the 1974-1975 global recession, most developing countries maintained strong growth rates, relying on large external capital flows to finance their growing current account deficits. Throughout the post-1973 period, average growth rates in the developing area were only 1 percentage point lower than in the sixties. But, unfortunately, the large external deficits experienced by these countries often reflected policy efforts to maintain consumption rather than to encourage investment.

I would point out, however, that the experience of many advanced developing countries was an exception to the overall LDC performance. These countries managed to outperform all other broad country groupings in the world economy. Their real growth rates in 1974-1979 were higher than in the preceding decade. They increased their export market shares in manufactured goods and were able to benefit from export-led growth. In general, their successful policy performance maintained international credit worthiness and encouraged continuing private capital flows that financed domestic investment.

But as a whole, policies in the developing world stressed financing rather than adjusting. As a result, substantial increases in external debt occurred without commensurate increases in capacity to service debt, and some of these countries now face actual or potential borrowing constraints. It is important that these countries initiate adjustment programs now, before their borrowing prospects deteriorate further. Clearly the basic economic restructuring that is needed in many cases will take time. But appropriate policies, formulated in conjunction with IMF and World Bank support, can point the way to lasting solutions and strengthen the prospects for continued financing while those solutions are in train.

The experience of the last several years in the areas of international adjustment is thus encouraging, if by no means altogether satisfactory. Short-term adjustments among the major oil-importing countries—the traditional focus of the adjustment process—have in fact been made with reasonable success, contributing to a more sustainable payments pattern and to overall monetary stability. The process of longer-term adjustment to a radically altered energy balance has begun, and promising results have already been recorded. Much more remains to be accomplished in this latter area and in overall adjustment, particularly by some developing countries, but I believe we can conclude that the adjustment process is on sound footing as we enter the 1980s.

## International Liquidity

This brings us to the more institutional aspects of the monetary system as it seems to be developing in the early 1980s. Our global monetary arrangements, along with the substantial adjustments in national balance-of-payments positions already addressed, have evolved effectively during a difficult period for the world economy. But the large imbalances of the past few years have themselves brought changes in international financing and liquidity, changes that pose important questions for the future operation of the system.

The private capital markets have played an extremely important role in the recycling process. In 1979, and so far in 1980, the private markets have once again proved to be flexible and imaginative in matching the needs of lenders and borrowers. Last year, record levels of new international financing were arranged. In total, private credits arranged in all maturity areas in fact substantially exceeded current financing needs. As a result, foreign exchange reserves of the oil importing areas increased. This cushion provided very important help earlier this year when capital markets were unusually turbulent. During the first quarter of 1980, both borrowers and lenders partially withdrew from the market. More recently, private credit flows have returned to levels more nearly comparable with borrowing requirements.

But we cannot rely exclusively on private markets. Some borrowers will face serious constraints on their access to private markets, and we must assure that official financing is available in adequate amounts to support required adjustment programs and maintain financial stability while adjustment is taking place.

The major expansion of demand for international financing over the last decade, and the satisfaction of that demand with a variety of currencies and innovative financing techniques, has changed the international monetary landscape. Indeed, some observers have been ready to announce that we have entered into a multicurrency reserve system. It is certainly indisputable that, over the last few years, we have been moving away from the virtual monopoly previously held by the U.S. dollar in the composition of international monetary reserves and use in trade and financial transactions. Other national currencies—particularly the German *mark* but also the Japanese *yen* and the Swiss *franc*—have clearly increased in importance.

The creation of the European Currency Unit (ECU) represents a further effort to develop alternative monetary instruments, in this case to meet the regional needs of the European Monetary System (EMS) for a settlement medium. The next phase of the EMS envisages an institutionalization of the ECU that would facilitate and strengthen European monetary integration. In time, the ECU could become an instrument capable of enabling European countries jointly to assume greater responsibility for meeting global credit needs.

Nevertheless, the trend toward the use of currencies other than the dollar has been considerably more gradual than casual impressions might suggest. Indeed, it has been less than might be implied by the relative reduction in the role of the U.S. economy and financial markets in global production and international transactions that has taken place over the years.

Estimates of the currency composition of world foreign exchange reserves can be obtained from data published by the IMF covering a substantial portion of its membership. The Fund data indicate that the dollar share of the reserves of these countries, calculated in special drawing rights (SDR), was about 78 percent at the end of last year, compared with almost 85 percent in early 1973.[1] While the data are only partial and interpretation is complicated by the effects of exchange rate changes on the calculations, the data do show a moderate decline in the dollar share of world reserves, though that share is still dominant.

The dollar also remains the predominant currency in international trade and the currency in which the major portion of international transactions are denominated. In 1979 about 60 percent of international bonds issued and some 95 percent of new medium-term Euro-credits were dollar denominated. So also were about 72 percent of all Euro-currency liabilities that were outstanding at the end of last year. Other currencies still play a much smaller international role than the dollar, even collectively and certainly so singly.

Thus a multicurrency system is by no means fully in being. Nevertheless, current trends point toward the evolution of such a system. Moreover, policy developments in several key countries may promote the trend. In the past, there has been a reluctance on the part of other major countries to accept a growing reserve role for their currencies. Recent actions and policy pronouncements in Germany, Japan, and Switzerland, however, indicate a greater degree of acquiescence and even interest in the development of larger reserve roles for their currencies, albeit in a gradual and controlled manner.

Such changes in attitude are fully understandable. As already noted, Germany and Japan moved into sizable current account deficit in 1979 and may remain in that position for some time to come. I earlier cited the elimination of their surpluses as a major achievement of the international adjustment process. At the same time, however, the emergence of sizable deficits required these countries to seek capital inflows to finance their new imbalances. The simplest and most natural way to do so was to offer investment opportunities in their own currencies, whose international role thus expanded substantially. Financing of payments deficits played a major role in the early evolution of the international use of sterling and the dollar, so we should not be surprised that one result of the recent shift in payments balances among the major countries would be an acceleration of the international use of other key currencies—especially the DM and the yen.

The other side of the new payments structure, of course, is the balance or surplus in the U.S. current account. The resultant strong performance of the dollar has removed much of the earlier motivation for moving out of dollars. The "diversification" motive was viewed a few years ago as a major factor encouraging increased use of other national currencies in international finance. Thus the increased international use of such currencies has become a bit more supply oriented than demand oriented.

If we are not yet in a full multicurrency system, but tending toward one, we should reflect on whether the trend is desirable or can and should be influenced. My own view is that a world monetary system based on several reasonably important national currencies might be subject to substantial risks and uncertainties and that the management of such a system might be more difficult than management of the present system. It is a matter of mathematics and logic that, given a matrix of options consisting of many currencies, the opportunities and motives for diversification and switching from one currency to another could grow. So too, could the potential instability and volatility of the system.

The risk is not confined simply to greater uncertainty and fluctuation of exchange rates. There is also a risk that, as a result of their greater international use, the exchange rates of individual key currencies could stray from levels that could reasonably be considered reflective of fundamental economic relationships.

We have seen such occurrences for the dollar. The existence of sizable dollar balances has probably contributed to excessive depreciation of our currency during periods when the underlying position was weakening (as in 1977-1978), and demand to build additional balances has probably contributed to excessive appreciation when the underlying position was strengthening (as in 1975-1976). The danger is that key currency countries—by definition, the most important countries in the monetary system—could be pressed by virtue of widespread international use of their currencies to retreat into controls and other devices to protect themselves from the operation of the exchange markets.

Lest there be misunderstanding, let me make clear that I am not advocating an effort to preserve excessive preeminence for the dollar. The United States is committed to the maintenance of a stable dollar and to a smooth adaptation of its future role in the international monetary system. But the United States has also been on record for some time as not opposing such gradual diminution of the role of the dollar as may be in line with changing circumstances in the global economy, as long as that evolution occurs in an orderly, nondisruptive manner.

Nor am I by any means denigrating the enhanced world position of other major currencies. Their increased use has met a clear demand and can be seen as one way to help spread the burden of defending the stability of the international monetary system. Indeed, I would expect that the use of nondollar national currencies will continue to grow, at least in absolute terms, for some time to come.

I am suggesting, however, that we should seek consciously to promote the use of the Special Drawing Right (SDR) as an alternative to the use of national reserve currencies. A monetary system relying increasingly on a managed international asset such as the SDR is likely to be more orderly than one based on several national currencies. Expanding the role and attractiveness of the SDR should thus be a major focus of our international monetary efforts in the period ahead.

**The SDR**

The IMF's Special Drawing Right facility was established by amendment of the Fund's Articles of Agreement in the late 1960s. In principle, the SDR was designed to meet a growing need for world reserves which would not be met through traditional sources. Stocks of gold and new gold production were physically limited and unrelated to the liquidity needs of the international monetary system. A strengthening of the U.S. balance of payments was expected to limit the availability of dollar reserves, and the system of par values and convertibility arrangements based on the dollar was in any case coming under increasing strain. Other currencies and nondollar capital markets played a relatively minor role in international financing. The SDR facility was thus seen as the vehicle for orderly creation of international reserves and for avoidance of the instabilities of a system increasingly dependent on gold or continued balance-of-payments deficits of the principal reserve center.

The international monetary system has undergone major transformation since those days. The par value, gold convertibility system of Bretton Woods has been replaced in the IMF Articles by provisions permitting flexible exchange rate arrangements. All significant monetary functions for gold have been eliminated. World capital markets and the availability of international financing from private sources have expanded enormously. But enhancing the SDR, and promoting its development as an important reserve asset, remains a desirable course for the system's evolution. In addition to its original purposes of avoiding undue reliance on gold and, especially, the dollar, the SDR now provides an alternative to unconstrained drift toward a potentially unstable multiple-currency system.

Indeed, the widespread desire to strengthen movement toward an SDR-base system has already contributed to renewed acceleration of the SDR's development:

Allocations have been resumed during the 1979-1981 "basic period," and allocations for the next basic period, beginning in 1982, will be considered by the IMF next spring.

The Fund has agreed to streamline the SDR currency basket from sixteen to five currencies, and to make it identical to the basket used for calculating the SDR interest rate, a step that should help considerably in making the SDR easier to understand and handle.

The list of official institutions authorized to hold, and deal in, SDRs has been widened to include the Swiss National Bank, the Bank for International Settlements, and a number of regional financial institutions.

Steps have been taken to greatly broaden the types of transactions countries can undertake in SDRs.

The possibility of IMF borrowing in private capital markets, now being explored by the IMF as a way of facilitating an expanded Fund role in the "recycling" process, opens new and potentially significant prospects for use of SDR-denominated instruments in private sector transactions. Some movement in this area has already been recorded with a number of SDR-denominated securities issues on international markets and, more recently, commercial bank offerings of SDR-denominated deposits.

Furthermore, these steps to improve the SDR should be pursued:

Increasing the interest rate on the SDR to the full market level.

Elimination of the remaining "reconstitution" requirement, which limits countries' ability to use their SDR allocations.

Initiation of studies by the IMF Executive Board on measures that could be taken to expand private sector use of SDR-denominated assets and liabilities.

Consideration by the World Bank of borrowing in SDR-denominated securities and making SDR-denominated loans, as the private market in SDRs develops and takes hold.

Use of the SDR denomination in the extension of export credits by our own Export-Import Bank and its foreign counterparts, which could help reduce predatory competition in this area as well as promote the role of the SDR.

Finally, we need to keep under study the feasibility of establishing in the IMF a Monetary Reserve Account (previously labelled a "substitution account") in which national currencies could be deposited in return for SDR-denominated assets. Interest in this idea has been distracted by the deficits created by the second oil shock and muted by the recent stability of the dollar. Nevertheless, the concept remains an attractive one in terms of future evolution toward a more stable SDR-centered monetary framework. An effectively functioning Monetary Reserve Account could substantially reduce the risks of a multiple-currency system by offering a way to convert existing official balances of national currencies without affecting the pattern of market exchange rates.

The effort to enhance the SDR's role as a major monetary instrument is a long-range task. But it offers significant potential for helping to develop a stable and orderly system in the future, an objective we must keep firmly in mind in designing our approaches to the more immediate problems that inevitably arise. It clearly represents the best prospect for channeling international monetary relations in a constructive and stabilizing direction.

**Management and Surveillance over the System**

At the beginning of this chapter, I described how the process of balance-of-payments adjustment has worked well in many respects in recent years. I also indicated the continuing need for longer-term adjustment to the fundamental changes that have taken place in the world economic and energy structure. The IMF therefore faces a major task over the next few years, both in facilitating the "recycling" process and in encouraging basic adjustments by its member countries.

There is not yet full understanding around the world of how rapidly the Fund is positioning itself to meet this new challenge. Access of its member countries to borrowing from the Fund is being expanded enormously. The duration of the IMF-supported adjustment programs is being lengthened, in recognition of the difficult structural adjustments faced by many borrowing countries. Greater emphasis is being placed on "supply side" considerations to generate investment and productivity growth.

As a result of all this, the Fund has worked out programs with member countries so far in 1980 which more than double the magnitudes of 1979. Despite the rhetoric heard occasionally from some, it is primarily the developing countries which are taking advantage of the Fund's progress in this particularly difficult period for them.

To position itself to do even more, the Fund is now completing implementation of a major increase in members' quotas—an increase which can be brought into effect as soon as congressional approval is completed, hopefully in the postelection session. The Fund is also exploring the possibility of augmenting its resources by borrowing directly from member countries—as it is doing to help via the Witteveen Facility in responding to current problems—and in the private capital markets.

From a somewhat longer-term perspective, it is important that the Fund strengthen its mechanisms for surveillance over the monetary system and the adjustment process in general. While international cooperation to make national economic policies compatible with internationally desirable objectives is intense, the process still lacks continuity and a framework of agreed goals and guidelines. It is important that, as the Fund works to develop the role of the SDR, it works in parallel, to strengthen the Fund's policies and procedures in the area of surveillance.

The Fund has adopted principles for the guidance of members in conducting exchange rate policy and procedures and criteria for use by the Fund in assessing members' policies. The guidelines and IMF practice recognize that surveillance cannot be confined to exchange rate policy, narrowly defined, but must encompass domestic policies as they affect the balance-of-payments adjustment process. The surveillance provisions give the IMF enhanced potential to advise not only countries in balance-of-payments deficit but also those in surplus on the international implications of their policies and on approaches they might appropriately follow to correct their payments imbalances.

These provisions give promise of a more symmetrical approach to the adjustment process, which is an important part of an effectively functioning system. The United States has advanced a number of proposals to strengthen the Fund's surveillance role:

> We believe it would be helpful for the Fund to assess the policies and performance of individual countries against a broadly agreed global economic framework.
>
> In promoting greater symmetry of adjustment, we believe the Fund should seek adjustment policy statements and analyses from any country experiencing a large payments imbalance, whether surplus or deficit.
>
> We have suggested that the IMF managing director be given greater freedom to initiate consultations with members where he has concerns about their policies.
>
> We believe the Fund should extend its surveillance to cover the appropriateness of countries' policies and plans for the financing of their payments imbalances; this would, of course, relate to the evolving international use of a variety of national currencies described earlier.

All these proposals involve sensitive aspects of national sovereignty and pride. While general agreement exists that IMF surveillance in some of these areas is useful, progress in strengthening surveillance has been slow, and the process is far from complete.

The process cannot be forced. But we must not confuse nominal sovereignty with real sovereignty. All of us live in a highly interdependent world economy and financial system. Effective collaboration must be fostered, or ineffective—even disruptive—governmental intervention will occur. It is important that we develop multilateral surveillance over the system if we want to insure that its evolution continues in a sound and rational direction.

## Conclusion

The international monetary system faces a range of difficult challenges as we enter the decade of the 1980s:

It must contend with the difficult adjustment problems facing its members and assure that adequate official balance-of-payments financing is available when the need arises.

It must address the potential problems of international liquidity management based on a multiplicity of national currencies.

It must promote an effective response to the need for greater coordination of national policies in an increasingly interdependent world.

The IMF is at the heart of the international community's efforts to meet these interrelated challenges in a coherent and effective way. Its financial resources are the world's principal source of official balance-of-payments financing and will be indispensable in promoting orderly and cooperative adjustment to new global energy and economic realities. The Fund's provisions on surveillance form a viable framework for coordinated international management of problems that increasingly appear on a global scale.

The United States has a major stake in successful resolution of these issues. The health of our own economy is tightly bound to that of the world economy. The share of trade in our GNP has doubled within the last decade. One out of seven U.S. manufacturing jobs and one out of three acres of U.S. farmland now produce for export. Almost $1 of every $3 of U.S. corporate profit derives from the international activities of American firms. The stability of our financial markets and the dollar depends importantly on maintenance of world financial and monetary stability.

Thus it is directly and clearly in our national self-interest that the International Monetary Fund succeed in its efforts to address these problems. This will not happen automatically or without strong support, financial and philosophical, from the United States and other IMF member countries.

The United States is giving the Fund strong support in its efforts to strengthen the role of the SDR and to develop IMF capabilities in overall supervision and management of the system. It is now crucially important that we participate in providing the financial support the Fund requires to perform the tasks we have assigned it via the Congress, when it returns in mid-November, taking the final step needed to permit U.S. participation in the pending quota increase.

The international monetary system has responded effectively to the unprecedented problems of the past decade. It has undergone two major changes—the move to flexible exchange rates and the creation of the SDR—which have enabled it both to meet those challenges and to position itself to deal with the equally difficult problems which lie ahead in the 1980s. We need now to build upon the successes of the past to assure that it will do so.

**Note**

1. If dollars that members of the European Monetary System have deposited for the European Currency Unit (ECU) are excluded from this calculation, the dollar's share in total reserves is smaller (some 65 percent at the end of last year), but that adjustment does not give a true picture since the dollars in question remain as underpinning for the ECU.

# 3 Recycling the World's Surpluses and Deficits: Challenge and Response

In the wake of the extremely large oil price increases since the end of 1978, world attention has turned again to the problem of recycling: the channeling of financing from the OPEC surplus countries to the large number of nations facing large, oil-induced balance-of-payments deficits. Many observers present the problem as both insoluble and devastating, portraying an international financial system that simply cannot handle the magnitude of financing required.

To be sure, there are certain aspects of recycling that are important cause for concern. We and other finance ministries around the world, and our colleagues in central banks, monitor the situation closely and are constantly considering whether our response mechanisms are adequate to handle it.

But two major points deserve much wider recognition than they have received. One is that recycling is clearly manageable for the foreseeable future and is being addressed actively and effectively by the international community. The second, which is even more fundamental, is that virtually all oil-importing countries, both industrialized and developing, appear to have learned the hard lesson that they must make fundamental adjustments to a radically changed world energy balance. This provides hope for a lasting resolution of the deeper economic problems manifested in the recycling issue. I would like to analyze the recycling issue comprehensively and in some detail, to see how great a challenge it presents and how the international financial community is responding to it.

## The Recycling Problem

What is the recycling problem? It is not a question of the availability of financing in any aggregate sense. The surpluses of the OPEC nations must by definition be invested somewhere in the oil-importing world. Hence the total amount of financing required by the oil-importing countries is automatically available in that aggregate sense. The problem is one of distribution and intermediation. If, for example, the OPEC nations accepted and held the local currency of each oil-importing country in payment

---

Originally presented on June 16, 1980, before the annual conference of the National Association of Accountants in New Orleans, Louisiana.

for oil, the oil imbalance would be automatically self-financing and there would be no recycling problem to worry about.

That, of course, is not the case. The OPEC nations take payment largely in dollars and—apart from direct aid to a relatively few developing countries—hold the bulk of their investments in the capital markets of the United States, other developed countries, and in the Euromarkets. The question is whether the financing represented by those investments will be redistributed in adequate amounts, and at appropriate maturities, to the individual countries facing the oil deficits in the first place. This will not occur automatically. Whether it occurs at all depends both on the ability of individual oil-importing countries to attract financing and on the institutional capability of the international financial system to intermediate on the scale required.

## The Pattern of Payments Imbalances

Let us progress quickly beyond theory to the facts of the situation. In 1980, we expect an OPEC current account surplus on the order of $120 billion.[1] All but one OPEC country (Algeria) is expected to be in surplus. Eighty percent of the total OPEC surplus will accrue to Saudi Arabia, Iraq, Kuwait, and the United Arab Emirates. The essence of recycling from the surplus side thus relates primarily to these countries.

The reemergence of a very large OPEC surplus—up from about $70 billion in 1979 and virtually zero in 1978—is in some ways reminiscent of the situation following the first major round of oil price increases, in 1973-1974. But there are key differences, negative and positive.

In the earlier period, the OPEC surplus peaked almost immediately (in 1974) and declined rapidly to nearly zero in four years. Such a scenario could happen again, but we cannot count on it. Given the relatively tight oil market conditions that may persist over the next few years, pressure on real oil prices may as well be upward as downward, in contrast to the decline in real oil prices during 1975-1978. Moreover, OPEC countries may not absorb their oil surpluses with increased imports as rapidly as in the earlier period.

We must therefore plan against the possibility of more sustained large current account imbalances over the next few years, with the OPEC surplus trending down much less rapidly than before. This suggests that *adjustment* must be a much more central component of the global response than in 1974-1975. Virtually all oil-importing countries will have to adjust both their energy policies and their macroeconomic policies in response to the higher oil prices themselves and to the inflationary and recessionary impact of these prices. Fortunately, most developed and developing countries are doing so.

Our own country is perhaps the most dramatic case in point: in 1974, the United States sought to reject totally the impact of higher oil prices on its economy by applying price controls to crude oil and the whole range of oil products; whereas we are now moving rapidly toward a full pass-through of the impact of world oil price increases and paying the inevitable, if hugely costly, price in terms of growth, inflation, and high unemployment.

The second important difference from post-1973 is that the pattern of current account deficits among the oil-importing nations is much less unstable from a financing point of view, at both aggregated and disaggregated levels.

The counterpart of the OPEC surplus of $120 billion is a deficit of around $70 billion in the industrialized countries and about $50 billion in the oil-importing developing countries. Hence, contrary to the general impression, financing requirements are not primarily focused on the less developed countries (LDCs) at least for 1980. In fact, the current account position of the Organization for Economic Cooperation and Development (OECD) countries as a group is expected to deteriorate by roughly $95 billion between 1978 and 1980, whereas that of the oil-importing developing countries will deteriorate by much less—about $25 billion.

Even more important is the distribution of the deficits among individual countries. In 1975-1976, a large portion of the OECD deficit was borne by the weaker economies of that time—particularly Britain and Italy, about which there was much loose (and foolish) talk of pending "national bankruptcy."

This time, however, over 40 percent of the OECD deficit is likely to be borne by the three strongest financial powers: Germany, Japan and, to a much lesser extent, the United States. Indeed, these three will probably account for more than one-quarter of the entire OPEC surplus. So a very large part of the increased global need for balance-of-payments financing will be borne by countries having the greatest underlying economic strength, holding a huge proportion of world reserves, and having the greatest ability to attract private capital, including, in the case of Germany and Japan, through efforts to promote international use of their currencies as investment media. This concentration of increased financing requirements on the strongest economies should be an important source of stability for the recycling process as a whole. The remainder of the OECD deficit is distributed widely, in relatively small amounts, across the other countries; only two (Norway and Switzerland) may be in small surplus. There are unlikely to be general financing problems in this group.

Among the "big three," the pattern of current account imbalances should also provide a basis for reasonable stability. Japan and Germany, following a period of very large current account surpluses and reserve accumulation, moved sharply into deficit in 1979 and 1980 and are expected to remain there in 1981. Conversely, the United States, after two years of large current account deficits, moved into balance in 1979 despite a huge increase in its oil import costs.

The recent oil price increases did produce a deficit in the first quarter of 1980, but the U.S. current account has probably been in sizable surplus for the last couple of months and will likely be in surplus for the whole of 1981. The overall picture of the U.S. external accounts, with the exception of the first quarter of this year, is one of rough balance or surplus over the three-year period 1979-1981. The imbalances among the three largest countries, which during 1976-1978 period were a major source of exchange market instability and disorder, will have been reversed during 1979-1981—indicating that the international adjustment process works. More broadly, it is clear that virtually all industrialized countries have undertaken important internal adjustment efforts—via new policies to reduce energy usage and increase energy production, slower economic growth, and (in some cases) new incentives to productive investment. There is thus a solid base upon which the recycling process can take place.

Although the global current account deterioration is heavily concentrated in the industrial countries, the developing nations nonetheless face financing requirements that are large, historically and in relation to the size of their economies. At the aggregate level, however, the problem is less ominous than it seems. During the past two years, these countries have built up their foreign exchange reserves by $25 billion. If they simply cease the reserve buildup, they therefore need not borrow more from private sources to finance their deficits in 1980 than they did last year—despite the higher level of the deficits. In essence, they wisely positioned themselves ahead of time.

Again, it is critical to disaggregate and look at individual countries. Within the LDC group, some thirteen countries rely heavily on private market financing; in fact, an even smaller group of about five countries has accounted for the lion's share of LDC borrowing in the private markets over the past few years. This group of thirteen "privately financed" developing countries is likely to account for almost half of the total LDC current account deficit this year and next. Their aggregate deficit of $24 billion in 1980 will represent a rough doubling from 1978.

However, it is these countries which experienced particularly large reserve increases in 1978 and 1979. Hence their need for private finance is no greater than in the past two years and could actually be a bit less. Moreover, most of them—for example, Brazil, Korea, the Philippines—have already initiated major efforts to adjust to the new situation and trim their deficits substantially. We expect that their access to needed levels of private finance will continue.

The other non-oil developing countries—that is, the vast majority of developing countries which do not have substantial access to the private financial markets—also face an increase in financing needs. The question facing these countries differs in character from that facing the OECD countries and the thirteen privately financed LDCs: whether donor countries—including (importantly) the OPEC countries—will increase official development assitance sufficiently to offset the sharply increased deficits. Fortunately, it appears that an increased level of aid will be forthcoming. If it is not adequate, cutbacks in growth and development programs are inevitable for a number of countries which are already very poor and growing very slowly.

My conclusion is that, even though a large OPEC surplus may persist for some time, the pattern of deficits and financing needs in the oil-importing world is sustainable for the foreseeable future. This does not mean that there will be no problems. Some individual countries, developed and developing alike, may well encounter financial difficulties and need to adjust further. But any such problems are likely to be selective; the pattern of imbalances should not pose major problems of financing in any aggregate sense. There are, moreover, a number of developments on the financing side that provide a basis for confidence that the system can continue to function with reasonable stability over the longer term as well.

## The International Financial Response

In the period following the 1973-1974 oil price increases, the private market met roughly three-fourths of the net financing requirements of deficit countries. The commercial banking system accounted for roughly half of the private total. Despite widespread questions at the beginning of the period about the capacity of the private banks to meet greatly expanded requirements, the system proved to be innovative and highly efficient in channeling financing to countries in need.

The private markets will again have to meet the bulk of world financing requirements. No other source is realistically available. Hence there are again questions about the willingness and ability of the private banking system to play the same major role in the process.

Given the large borrowings and debt accumulations that have taken place in recent years and the prospect of several years of sizable financing needs, these questions must be taken seriously. On the other hand, there are a number of positive factors in the financing outlook. I would list four in particular.

First, the banks' experience with international lending, in terms of profits and repayment records, has compared favorably with that on domestic loans. Particularly in a period of relative slack in domestic credit demand—strong domestic growth is not projected for the OECD countries in the next few years—the banks may continue to see substantial attraction in foreign lending. Modest increases in spreads for some borrowers should help to compensate for increases in perceived risk. Undisbursed commitments for bank loans remain substantial, and a number of countries with large bank debt have adopted adjustment programs that should strengthen their external positions and assessments of their creditworthiness. The private banking system may understandably be cautious; the role of individual banks in the process may change, with some taking a larger share and others proceeding more slowly for a while; but none of this suggests that the banking system as a whole will withdraw, or even retreat, from the recycling process.

Second, despite the obituary notices widely posted several months ago, the bond markets are alive and may well play an increasingly significant role in the recycling process. Investors, particularly governments and institutions with sizable positions, appear to be moving toward widening their portfolios of investment assets both geographically and with respect to maturity. Indeed, the concentration of financing requirements in the developed countries may well favor bond financing. The recovery of the bond markets should stand to benefit developing countries as well. Largely excluded from these markets a decade ago, LDCs raised some $3 billion through placements of foreign and international bond issues in 1979, a trend that indicates an increased willingness to accept new names and less familiar risks, at least selectively.

Third, a substantial part—some $45 billion—of foreign borrowing by the developing countries since 1975 has been used not to finance current account deficits but to build up reserves. This more than doubling of reserves represents a very substantial potential source of financing for these countries in the period ahead, suggesting less pressure on financial markets than might be implied by the current account figures alone. Indeed, as already noted, if the developing countries simply stopped borrowing to build up reserves during 1980, their total recourse to the financial markets would not need to expand despite the sharp increase in their current account financing requirements.

## The Role of the IMF and World Bank

Fourth, and perhaps most importantly from the longer-term perspective, the public international financial institutions are positioning themselves to play a significantly larger role in dealing with the large payments imbalances over the next few years. The International Monetary Fund and the World Bank—the institutions that played so fundamental a role in the cooperative effort to rebuild the world economy following World War II—are now preparing to play an equally central role in the task of structural adjustment that faces the world economy today.

These institutions have two key functions to perform in the recycling process. The first is the provision of official balance-of-payments financing. The second, more innovative and reflecting the fundamental lesson of the past decade, is the promotion of basic structural adjustment by borrowing countries to accommodate the dramatic changes that have taken place in the world economy. In addition to dealing directly with the most critical economic problems faced by borrowing countries, this encourages increased private financing to flow to those countries in recognition of the improved creditworthiness which results from Fund and/or Bank programs.

Recourse to the IMF has increased sharply, with new programs agreed to or in prospect during the first half of 1980—about $4 billion—already double the level throughout all of 1979. This trend seems likely to continue. To encourage this, the IMF is making a number of changes in its lending policies in recognition of the structural nature of many of the adjustment needs faced by its member countries:

It plans to shift the emphasis of its adjustment programs to greater concentration on productive investment and *stimulation of supply* in borrowing countries, while attaining overall financial balance.

It is prepared to *lengthen the period* of its adjustment programs to accommodate the need for structural change.

It is also prepared to *expand members' access to its resources* in appropriate cases, and has now lent as much as 600 percent of a country's quota.

The IMF's financial position is very strong at present, and it will receive a further injection of resources with implementation of a 50 percent increase in quotas by the end of 1979. The Supplementary Financing Facility, which was negotiated in 1977 and whose U.S. participation was approved by the Congress in 1978, is now being used quite actively. To assure that the Fund remains in a position to meet the needs of its members during a period of potential strain, the IMF's Interim Committee in April authorized the IMF managing director to explore the possibility of IMF borrowing from potential lenders—that is, surplus OPEC countries—in the event a need for additional resources arises. We expect that those countries will cooperate in positioning the Fund to play an even greater role in the financing and adjustment process if the need arises.

These efforts by the IMF closely parallel a major initiative being undertaken by the World Bank to support structural adjustment in the developing nations. With strong support from the United States, the Bank has initiated a new program of nonproject, medium-term lending whose disbursement would be conditional on specified economic policy changes by the borrowing country designed to produce structural adjustment—especially in response to the energy situation—in its economy. These loans would, like all Bank activities, contribute to the long-run development of the recipient country. In addition, however, their nonproject nature and much faster rate of disbursement would help smooth the recycling process. In developing and implementing such loans, the Bank will work closely with the Fund. This effort is yet another demonstration—like the shift to basic human needs lending in the earlier 1970s and energy lending in the late 1970s—of the speed and flexibility with which the World Bank can respond to major world economic problems.

Although the Bank's structural adjustment lending program has just begun, we see a potentially major role for the institution in facilitating the recycling-cum-adjustment process for its developing member countries. Fortunately, the Bank too is well positioned to finance these and its other programs. The member countries have agreed to a general capital increase of $40 billion, which will double the Bank's lendable resources, and to a replenishment of the International Development Association—its concessional lending window—by $12 billion for the period 1980-1983.

Both key institutions are thus in a solid financial position and can respond quickly and flexibly as their members' needs evolve in the period ahead. Their efforts, not only to complement the recycling process but to facilitate adjustment by their members to the deeper structural problems, represent a most important—and most promising—contrast with the experience of the earlier period of oil-induced payments imbalances.

These adjustments will not be easy, particularly in a period of relatively slow world economic growth. They will necessarily take time, as reflected in the adaptations being made in the institutions' lending policies. But the adjustments must be initiated—and the deficits not simply financed—if lasting economic and financial stability is to be restored.

The world has experienced two major shocks during the past decade arising fundamentally from its excessive dependence on oil. Each shock has brought steep inflation, depressed economic activity, and international financial strain. The world faces perhaps frequent repetition of these shocks in the future unless it begins, in a purposeful and concerted way, to undertake the basic changes that are needed. This lesson appears to have been learned. It is embodied in the reorientation of lending policies being undertaken by the IMF and World Bank and provides a strong basis for confidence that the world can and will deal with its basic economic problems.

### The Impact on the International Monetary System

Before concluding, let me address a related but somewhat longer-term question posed by the large scale of international financing now in prospect.

During the 1970s, international transactions and world reserves increased enormously. Although we do not have data for the currency composition of all transactions, the dollar clearly continued to play a dominant role. Indeed, the dollar's share in world official reserve holdings remained stable throughout most of the decade. In future years, the dollar will continue to play a major role in international financing.

But there are reasons to expect that other currencies might begin to take on a growing role. In particular, the emergence of large deficits in Japan and Germany has already led to an expansion of foreign holdings of yen and Deutschemarks as those countries endeavor to finance their deficits. As a result, attitudes in those countries toward international use of their currencies seems to be growing more positive. Coupled with the development over the years of highly efficient financial markets outside the United States, this should mean that other countries and currencies could begin to assume a greater part of the responsibility for meeting world financing requirements in the period ahead.

In addition, the IMF's Special Drawing Right is assuming a larger role in world reserve holdings. Allocations have resumed during 1979-1981. The increase in IMF quotas and the prospective increase in IMF financing will be denominated in SDRs. Borrowing by the IMF, should that prove necessary, would give SDR-denominated assets an even more direct role in the recycling process and a more prominent position in world reserves.

The international reserve system is thus evolving toward a greater multiplicity of currencies (or currency "baskets," such as the SDR and the European Currency Unit). In many respects this is a healthy and positive development, which implies less concentrated pressure on individual currencies and on the system. On the other hand, a multicurrency system could prove to be unstable, as both the implied freedom of financial markets and the experience of investors with holding a variety of assets increase the potential for shifts from one to another.

Such considerations underlie the continuing effort to develop the role of the SDR as an increasingly important, internationally created and managed reserve asset. The reemergence of large payments deficits and financing needs has diverted present attention from these longer-term considerations to more immediate and pressing questions. Yet these longer-term issues will reappear when more immediate concerns are dealt with, and we believe that it is important for the IMF to keep these questions of the longer-term evolution of the monetary system near the top of its agenda.

Regardless of the direction of the system's evolution, the dollar will continue to play a key role in the international financial markets for the foreseeable future. This means that the United States must pursue policies that will sustain confidence in the dollar. It is the intention and basic thrust of our policies—to control inflation, secure energy independence, and restore vitality to the U.S. economy. The achievement of rough balance on surplus in the U.S. current account over the three-year period 1979-1981 will support this effort.

## Conclusion

Despite the reemergence of unprecedented world payments imbalances and the likelihood that they will remain with us for some time, the prospects for the recycling process are relatively good.

For the near term, the pattern of current account deficits and financing needs is broadly consistent with orderly financing through the private markets. In addition, the international institutions stand ready and equipped to play an increased role in the process if and as that becomes necessary.

From a somewhat longer perspective, the size and pattern of payments deficits and financing needs is necessarily less clear. But the international community appears to accept the need for fundamental structural change—to avoid perpetual, destructive reliance on imported oil. This is the essence of the real solution to the recycling problem for the longer term. Here, too, the international institutions are prepared to exercise guiding influence.

The international community is moving forcefully on both the financing and adjustment fronts. It will monitor the situation carefully as it evolves, and be prepared to reply flexibly to changing needs. There is a clear challenge. We are designing an effective response.

## Note

1. All numbers used in this presentation *include* official transfers, which are relatively stable and thus should be included before drawing a "bottom line" for payments imbalances and financing needs. Officials of the International Monetary Fund frequently *exclude* such transfers in calculating imbalances; this difference (together with some different definitions of country groupings) accounts for virtually all the difference between our figures and theirs.

# 4 The Role of the International Monetary Fund

This is a time of severe strain in the world economy. Recent developments both at home and abroad have made it necessary for us in the United States to intensify our antiflation fight. We do so with total resolve, for I am sure that we all share an awareness that failure to get inflation under control could have ominous implications not only for our economy but for our society as a whole.

The challenges of inflation are not faced by the United States alone. Soaring inflation—and the concomitant problems of slow growth, low productivity, high interest rates and external payments imbalances—are worldwide phenomena. During the last two reporting months, wholesale price increases in Japan, Great Britain, and Italy have all exceeded an annual rate of 25 percent. Even in West Germany, a country with a remarkable postwar record of price stability, the inflation rate in wholesale prices is now at the double-digit level.

These somber developments come at a time when there is already considerable political and economic strain—in the international community. The tension immediately affecting our political interests is most clearly linked to events in Southwest Asia. The revolution in Iran and the Soviet aggression in Afghanistan have heightened awareness througout the world of the many different sources of threats to peace and prosperity.

Just as our response to developments in Southwest Asia requires coordination with our allies, so must our response to the rampant inflation and other economic problems that the world now faces be coordinated internationally. As a complement to the domestic measures which the administration is now taking, we must take steps to strengthen the international monetary system. The most effective instrument to promote a strong, stable international financial structure and to deal with inflation and our other serious economic problems on a worldwide basis is the International Monetary Fund.

As the worldwide inflation problem indicates, the global economic outlook as we enter the 1980s is not favorable. The 1970s were already characterized by unprecedented economic problems. Largely as a result of various cooperative efforts, the international community weathered the economic turbulence reasonably well. Nevertheless, adverse oil market

Originally presented on March 31, 1980, before the Subcommittee on International Finance of the Senate Committee on Banking, Housing and Urban Affairs.

developments have again radically affected economic prospects. The reemergence of a large current account surplus in the OPEC countries and the inevitable generation of a corresponding deficit in the oil-importing world will make serious balance-of-payments pressures inevitable for a growing number of countries.

At present, we anticipate an OPEC current account surplus of about $120 billion in 1980, and current account deficits, after official transfers, of about $70 and $50 billion for the OECD and LDCs (less developed countries) respectively. A world environment of slower growth, high inflation, heightened caution in the private financial sector, and continuing threat of energy supply disruptions will simultaneously make the financing of external deficits and the adjustment of national economies to reduce those deficits more difficult. The private financial sector will again meet the bulk of expanding international financing needs as there is no other source for the magnitudes that will be required. Flows of official development assistance will continue to rise. But we have to anticipate that a number of countries, developed and developing, will encounter growing financial difficulties and pressures to adjust and bring their external positions closer into line with sustainable flows of financing.

**Role of the IMF**

A strong and effective IMF is critical to our effort to assure world monetary and financial stability and to provide the broad cooperative framework we will need to overcome fundamental economic difficulties.

The IMF serves two related functions—general guidance over the operations and evolution of the monetary system and provision of temporary balance of payments financing.

First, its Articles of Agreement constitute the operating rules of the international monetary system and establish member countries' obligations to promote a cooperative and stable world monetary order. The decade of the seventies brought major changes in the international monetary system and in the IMF's role in guiding the system's operations.

In the area of balance-of-payments adjustment, the Bretton Woods par value exchange rate obligations have been replaced by obligations on members to pursue policies to achieve the underlying economic stability needed for genuine and sustained exchange rate stability. The IMF has been given the task of surveillance over members' compliance with those obligations, and over the operations of the balance-of-payments adjustment process more generally.

In the area of international liquidity the IMF membership has established the objective of making the Special Drawing Right (SDR) the principal reserve asset in the international monetary system.

These changes are not abstractions. They have paralleled and to a large extent have reflected changes in the position and role of the dollar in the system. The original Bretton Woods arrangements assumed a fixed and central role for the dollar, with the U.S. position essentially passive and the product of other countries' actions in pursuing their own balance-of-payments policies and objectives. That arrangement ultimately became both unsustainable and intolerable in terms of U.S. economic interests. The new arrangements have provided much more scope for balance-of-payments adjustment by the United States and recognize the need for greater symmetry in encouraging appropriate adjustments by all nations—those in surplus as well as those in deficit.

At the same time, the world's reserve system has been undergoing significant change. Increases in the relative economic size and financial capacity of other major countries have tended to lead to some growth in the use of their currencies in international transactions and reserves. On the one hand, such a development can help to mitigate some of the burdens on the dollar and U.S. financial markets that arose from its extremely large international role. On the other hand, the process of change can itself be unsettling and disruptive, and there is a widespread view that increasing reliance on an internationally created and managed reserve instrument such as the SDR would be preferable to development of a multiple-currency reserve system, with its inherent potential for large and abrupt shifts among alternative currencies. The IMF over the past few years has taken a number of important steps to promote the role of the SDR, and is presently considering a potentially significant further step in its examination of the proposed Substitution Account.

The proposed Substitution Account would be affiliated with the IMF and would accept deposits of dollars—and in time, perhaps other currencies—by foreign central banks in exchange for claims denominated in Special Drawing Rights. The Account would invest its dollar holdings in interest-earning U.S. government securities and would pay interest to the holders of the SDR-denominated claims.

A properly designed Account could foster greater stability in the monetary system by providing an internationally agreed, nondisruptive mechanism for countries to diversify reserve portfolios and by strengthening the SDR's role in official reserves. Discussions on the Account are progressing, although a number of major issues have not yet been resolved. Key among these issues is the question of assuring financial balance in the Account. A consensus appears to be emerging on use of a portion of the IMF's gold holdings as an equitable, internationally shared means of assuring the Account's financial position.

Some use of IMF gold to help promote the role of the SDR would be supportive of, not inconsistent with, the continued reduction of the monetary role of gold. It would serve to promote the role of the SDR as the world reserve system evolves. It would involve no transactions in gold among monetary authorities and no addition to countries' gold holding. And it could, if there were an actual need to use the gold to help balance the Account's financial position, result in further disposal of monetary gold on the private markets.

We have no firm view on the optimal size of the Account. It might well begin with relatively modest amounts and grow over time. Clearly, it should be large enough and attract broad enough participation to be a meaningful step forward in the role of the SDR, but these criteria are difficult to quantify and will require further discussion. Participation in the Account would be voluntary, both because real progress in developing the SDR's role requires genuine commitment on the part of IMF members and because there will be no way to compel countries to participate anyway.

Even with a Substitution Account and other steps to enhance the role of the SDR, the dollar remains critically important to the operation of the international monetary system, and the U.S. economy remains a powerful element of that system. This will continue to be the case, and we recognize and accept the responsibilities incumbent on the United States to maintain a sound economic position and stable dollar. The recent comprehensive measures announced by the President to combat inflation reflect our firm commitment to these objectives.

The second basic function of the IMF, closely tied to its role in guiding the overall operation of the system, is the provision of temporary financing in support of members' efforts to deal with their balance-of-payments problems in a manner that is not destructive of national or international prosperity—and thus to promote a smoothly functioning world payments system in the context of a strong and stable international economy. This is a central objective of the IMF, and one in which all must participate as an obligation of IMF membership.

The IMF is essentially a revolving fund of currencies, provided by every member and available to every member for temporary balance-of-payments financing under prescribed criteria. Each country is obligated to provide its currency to the IMF to finance drawings by other countries facing balance-of-payments needs; and each country in turn has a right to draw upon the IMF in case of balance-of-payments need. When a country provides financing to the IMF—that is, when its currency is drawn from the Fund—it receives an automatic and unchallengeable right to draw that amount from the IMF in usable foreign exchange. This is the so-called reserve position in the IMF, an automatically available reserve claim on the IMF which is normally carried in countries' international monetary reserves.

Financing thus flows back and forth through the IMF depending on balance-of-payments patterns and financing requirements at any given time. There is no fixed class or group of lenders or borrowers, no concept of "donor" or "recipient" in the IMF. It is not an aid institution. All major industrial countries have drawn upon the IMF at times. Many members, developed and developing alike, have been on both sides of the financing and drawing ledger during the history of their participation. In fact, while the U.S. quota subscription has been drawn upon many times over the years, our own drawings on the IMF, totaling some $7.5 billion, are the second largest of the entire membership.

**Proposed Increase in Quotas**

Quotas are central in the IMF. Members' quota subscriptions constitute the IMF's permanent financial resources. Quotas determine both the amount of IMF resources a member can draw when in balance-of-payments need and its obligation to provide resources when its balance-of-payments is strong. Quotas determine the distribution of SDR allocations, and, of key importance, voting power. Unlike the case in many institutions, where member countries try to hold down their shares of participation, countries compete to gain the largest possible share of the total in the IMF because of the financing and votes that a larger quota share provides.

To ensure that IMF quotas remain realistic and adequate, they are reviewed periodically in relation to the growth of international transactions, the size of payments imbalances and financing needs, and world economic prospects. Such a review was initiated in 1977, and led to a resolution adopted by the IMF Board of Governors on December 11, 1978, with the U.S. governor concurring, calling for an increase in overall IMF quotas by 50 percent, raising total quotas from about SDR 39 billion to roughly SDR 58 billion. The increase proposed for the U.S. quota amounts to SDR 4,202.5 million, equivalent to about $5.3 billion at current exchange rates. This increase would raise the U.S. quota by 50 percent, from SDR 8,405 million (or about $10.6 billion) to SDR 12,607.5 million (or about $15.9 billion).

The negotiation of quota shares is always difficult, with pressures on the United States to accept a smaller quota share. Given the key roles of the dollar and the U.S. economy in the international monetary system, and the IMF's central role in guiding the operations and evolution of the system, it is essential that the U.S. maintain an appropriate share of quotas and votes, and thus its influence over basic decisions about the system. In the end, the pressures for a reduced U.S. share were successfully resisted during the most recent review, and only a very few selective changes in quota shares were agreed.

The decision to propose a 50 percent overall increase in quotas reflected a widely felt view that quotas had, by any measure, failed to keep pace with potential balance-of-payments financing needs. Despite quota increases on four occasions during the IMF's history, aggregate quotas had fallen to about 4 percent of annual world imports, in comparison with 8 to 12 percent during the 1960s and 10 to 14 percent during the 1950s. The adequacy of quotas had eroded particularly during the seventies, as the ratio of quotas to members' aggregate current account deficits fell by two-thirds between 1971-1973 and 1978. In mid-1978 the Fund's usable quota resources—that is, its holding of the currencies of members then in strong payments positions—totaled only about SDR 16 billion, or just over 1 percent of world imports. In November 1978, before the Supplementary Financing Facility was put in place, the amount of usable quota resources was effectively halved to around SDR 8 billion, when the United States drew the equivalent of $3 billion, and the dollar was taken off the IMF's "budget" of currencies used in financing current drawings.

These shifts in the IMF's "liquidity" illustrate the difficulties of projecting either the level of usable IMF resources or the level of future drawings on the Fund. In its 1977 quota review, the IMF estimated that the level of international transactions between 1978 and 1983 would increase by 60 percent in SDR terms. In fact, that 60 percent figure is now much too low as inflation, oil price increases, and other factors have caused a much more rapid expansion in the value of world trade and financial transactions. And, even if we could accurately predict future levels of world trade, we would not know the pattern of trade, the size and distribution of payments imbalances, or the availability of financing from banks and other sources.

In determining how a large quota increase would be needed, it was recognized that the IMF's Supplementary Financing Facility would be phased out after a two- to three-year period. That Facility, for which U.S. participation was approved by Congress late in 1978, has proved to be an extremely important temporary reinforcement of IMF resources during a period of growing financial strain. The Facility began operation in early 1979 on the basis of financial commitments amounting to about SDR 7.8 billion. OPEC countries are providing over 40 percent of the total with Saudi Arabia the largest single participant. To date, the Facility has been used in conjunction with IMF programs totaling about $3 billion and is assisting a wide variety of countries of special interest to the United States—including Turkey, Peru, Korea, the Philippines, and Sudan—in dealing with severe payments difficulties. A number of countries are now discussing with the IMF programs under the Facility, and total use before the Facility expires (scheduled for early 1981 or 1982) should be substantial. This Facility, designed as a temporary bridge to the quota increase now in process, is a timely and valuable source of support for the Fund's operations in this period, and congressional approval for it has proven to be extremely wise.

It was in the light of these considerations that the IMF membership concluded that a 50 percent increase in total quotas would be the minimum required to assure that the IMF remained in a strong position to meet prospective needs. Even a 50 percent increase will do little more than temporarily halt the decline in the relative size of IMF resources into the mid-1980s. In fact, most developing countries and some OECD members, fearing growing world economic uncertainties, pressed hard for a much larger increase.

Events since completion of the quota review have strengthened the need for the quota increase. Oil market developments have again substantially altered economic prospects and drawn the world into a pattern of sizeable payments imbalances. Countries must, and will begin adjusting to these developments, and that will cause further changes in world balance-of-payments patterns and financing needs that cannot now be foreseen. Moreover, events in Iran and Afghanistan have created a climate of concern and uncertainty that makes it all the more important to have in place the institutional means for assuring monetary stability and providing advice and financial support to countries facing the growing economic and financial problems of the 1980s.

The IMF must have adequate resources—and this means adequate quotas—to encourage countries to adjust in an appropriate way, rather than adopt trade and capital restrictions, aggressive exchange rate policies, or unduly restrictive domestic measures in order to reduce their financing needs. Such restrictive measures could have serious implications for the entire world economy and the prosperity of all nations, as well as for the economy of the country introducing them. We must not forget the lessons of the 1930s, when serious economic troubles were worsened by ultimately self-defeating actions of nations trying individually to preserve employment and prosperity during times of economic distress and international tension.

The impact on the United States today could be especially harmful. Our economy has grown heavily reliant on world trade and financial flows. An interdependent world brings real economic benefits, but also greater vulnerability to outside developments. Imported goods, from raw materials to high-technology products, are integrated into all phases of U.S. economic activity. Export markets constitute a major source of demand for U.S. goods and services. One out of every seven U.S. manufacturing jobs, and one out of every three acres of U.S. agricultural land produce for export. One out of every $3 of U.S. corporate profits comes from foreign operations (exports and investments). For the U.S. economy specifically and the world economy generally, prosperity is dependent on a well-functioning international financial system.

Uncertainties about the magnitude, distribution, and financing of payments imbalances over the next few years make it impossible to project the precise amount of IMF resources that will be used during the next five years. But we must assure ourselves that the IMF's resources are sufficient to meet its important responsibilities—measured against historic standards, current trends, and a realistic appreciation of the dangers we face as we enter a new decade.

**IMF Conditionality**

A crucial issue is whether IMF conditionality policies should be changed to prevent conflict with the fulfillment of the basic human needs of countries drawing on the Fund. This is one of the most important and least understood aspects of IMF assistance to its member countries. Conditionality is not designed to change the basic character of a member's economy, nor interfere in its sociopolitical evolution, nor punish the country for economic mismanagement. The central purpose of conditionality is to permit the IMF to encourage the adoption of policies which will correct the economic difficulties that resulted in balance-of-payments problems and the need for Fund financing in the first place.

It is important to remember that, whatever the cause of a country's balance-of-payments problem, unless it is temporary and self-reversing, the country will ultimately have to adjust. It cannot indefinitely spend reserves and borrow abroad. Without policy adjustments, the country's creditworthiness and ability to borrow abroad will inevitably decline, trade credit will evaporate, investment will generally fall, and growth will decline or become negative. This in itself is one form of adjustment, but it is harsh and inefficient. What may look like the easy way out is in fact very costly, and can make the return to sound economic growth an extremely difficult and slow process.

Most governments will make policy adjustments before the situation deteriorates to that extreme, but sometimes a country will not approach the Fund until the situation is desperate. This is a key point to remember. The Fund does not *cause* the lack of foreign exchange that interrupts vitally needed imports. Indeed the IMF, often alone, tries to help by providing resources to maintain the economy and balance of payments temporarily, and by providing policy advice to restore economic stability and sustained growth.

However, in return for this financing, the world community expects the government to foreswear measures disruptive to the world economy. To assure repayment, and the most beneficial results for the country, the Fund requires that the member undertake appropriate measures to solve its balance-of-payments problems. The adjustments that have to be made often involve short-term retrenchment—with or without the IMF. With the IMF, a short-term period of belt-tightening is more likely to be orderly and effective. If a country has gotten into very serious problems, and is spending far beyond what it can produce or finance on a sustainable basis, there will have to be cutbacks. These may well affect virtually all segments of the population. This is painful. But there is also pain and harm—perhaps much greater harm to the poorest—in letting a pervasive and destructive inflation and/or an external imbalance go unchecked, reducing real national incomes, permanently distorting consumption and investment patterns, and eroding the basic productive capability of the economy. If a Fund program can help establish a functioning base for growth and development, then the longer-term social and economic benefits can far outweigh any shorter-term costs.

Requests for IMF financing are initiated by the member country, and the precise type of financing and its terms are settled through discussions between the member government's representatives and the IMF. Each member proposes its own stabilization program in support of its financing request. The Fund does not insist on a particular method of adjustment and recognizes that economic structure and circumstances differ among members.

The Fund takes this approach for practical and philosophical reasons. It is appropriate for the IMF to say how much adjustment a country should undertake as a condition for obtaining financing, and establish overall targets for monetary growth, the budget deficit, and other macroeconomic variables. But the IMF should not tell a country whether it must cut military expenditures or social programs, or that it must tax this and subsidize that, or cut employment here and expand it there. These detailed implementing decisions must be made by the government concerned. It is highly unlikely that the United States would ever accept such interference with U.S. sovereignty. Neither would other countries.

There are various policy combinations which would permit a country to meet the targets negotiated with the IMF, so the member presumably chooses one that most conforms to its particular circumstances and objectives. Of course the IMF may well have views of what are efficient and equitable policy mixes and can discuss these with a prospective borrower if appropriate. There are cases where the Fund staff has advised against certain actions because of their likely social costs. The United States has, on a number of occasions, urged the Fund to suggest programs to governments that are conducive to development and social goals, while meeting overall economic requirements. But in the end the individual government is responsible for its own stabilization program—both in design and implementation—even though the IMF is often made the scapegoat for unpopular choices.

However, within these very real constraints, the IMF is making a continuing effort to improve and better adapt itself to the needs of its members.

First, reflecting the generally increased scale and persistence of balance-of-payments problems, the IMF now provides more financing for longer periods for nations with adjustment problems. Quota limits on drawings have been expanded and, for drawings with higher conditionality in the upper credit tranches, two- and three-year programs have become much more the accepted rule, in contrast to the one-year program that was traditional in earlier days.

In addition, a variety of IMF facilities are now available to members, ranging from unconditional reserve tranche drawings through facilities such as the Compensatory Financing Facility and the first credit tranche (both with relatively "light" conditionality requirements) to the upper credit tranche and Extended Fund Facility drawings. Of total drawings amounting to nearly $30 billion since 1973, roughly two-thirds has been drawn from unconditional or relatively unconditional facilities. Some countries have, of course, gotten into more serious difficulty and have had to turn to the more conditional facilities—which have themselves been expanded and adapted—and these are the cases one hears about most often. But it is important to bear in mind the whole spectrum of IMF financing facilities when assessing its role in balance-of-payments financing and adjustment.

Second, the IMF in 1979 undertook a major review of conditionality and established a new set of guidelines. To an extent the new guidelines formalize certain protections for borrowing countries that had already existed in practice, but they also add important new features. For example, they now emphasize the desirability of encouraging countries to adopt corrective measures at an early stage—before very severe adjustment policies may be needed—and recognize the need for more gradual and more flexible adjustment over longer periods. They also recognize that adjustment measures frequently encompass sensitive areas of national policy, and provide that in helping to devise adjustment programs the Fund will pay due regard to the domestic social and political objectives, the economic priorities and the circumstances of members, including the causes of their balance-of-payments problems. They provide that "performance criteria" will normally be confined to macroeconomic variables (other than those performance criteria needed to implement specific provisions of the articles, such as the avoidance of exchange restrictions). The new guidelines should help dispel the idea of conditionality as a weapon for imposing unnecessary hardships—and make clear that for countries with severe imbalances, adequate and timely adjustment, the objective of IMF conditionality, is in the best interests of both the individual country involved and the world community.

The third change in the IMF's approach to adjustment, and a particularly important one, is one stressed earlier—its new role in surveillance. Surveillance over every IMF member's efforts to foster orderly underlying economic and financial conditions provides valuable IMF leverage for promoting sound adjustment policies by all countries, surplus or deficit, whether or not they draw on the IMF's resources. It is designed to introduce a badly needed symmetry to the international monetary system, more effectively encouraging adjustment efforts by surplus countries, and not leaving the entire burden of adjustment on deficit countries. Development of IMF surveillance can be helpful in various ways. To the extent it encourages *earlier* adjustment action, it helps to avoid the more severe corrective measures which become necessary as a country's situation worsens; and to the extent it encourages adjustment action by *all* countries with large imbalances, it reduces the relative emphasis on those deficit countries drawing upon the IMF.

Thus the IMF is making a continuing effort to adapt to the changing needs and circumstances of its members. This process should, and will, continue. But as we move to adapt IMF policies and practices, we need to keep the IMF's basic purposes clearly in view and ensure that its programs do, in fact, effectively promote adjustment by its members. This is in the individual borrower's own interests and of the international community as well.

## IMF and the Budget

Before concluding this discussion of the IMF, let me mention the question of the budget and appropriations treatment of this quota increase. The president's budget submitted in January proposed that a program ceiling on the increase be provided in an appropriations act. We have been consulting extensively on this question with interested committees, and it appears that considerable interest is developing in an alternative approach which would involve the following:

> Appropriations would be required in the full amount of the increase, and that sum would be included in budget authority totals for fiscal year 1981.
>
> Payment of the quota increase would result in budgetary outlays as cash transfers are actually made to the IMF on the U.S. quota obligation.
>
> Simultaneously with any cash transfer, an offsetting budgetary receipt, representing an increase in the U.S. reserve position in the IMF, would be recorded.
>
> As a consequence of these offsetting transactions, transfers to and from the IMF under the quota obligations, therefore, would not result in net outlays or receipts.
>
> Net outlays or receipts resulting from exchange rate fluctuations in the dollar value of the SDR-denominated U.S. reserve position in the Fund would be reflected in the Federal budget. These net changes cannot

be projected and thus would be recorded only in actual budget results for the prior year.

We are continuing our consultations on this matter. The point I would stress is that under either the program ceiling in the president's budget or this alternative approach, U.S. payments on its quota subscription would not affect net budget outlays or the federal deficit.

## Conclusion

In conclusion, I would like to reemphasize my strong conviction that the Fund is essential to U.S. interests. The proposed quota increase is important for a number of reasons.

From the point of view of the international monetary system as a whole, it will help assure that the IMF can continue to meet its responsibilities for international monetary stability in a period of strain, danger, and financial uncertainty. From the point of view of individual countries, it will provide additional resources to encourage constructive balance-of-payments adjustment policies—and I note that IMF resources have been of major direct benefit to the United States when we faced severe balance-of-payments pressures. From the point of view of the United States, it maintains our financial rights and our voting share in the institution during a time when far-reaching changes in the monetary system—for example, a substitution account—are under consideration.

The record of the IMF is a good one in adapting to changing world circumstances and responding to the needs of its members. The proposed quota increase will provide the Fund with resources needed for its valuable work, and I urge the Committee to approve this legislation.

# Part III
# The United States in World Trade

# 5 The Growing International Competitiveness of the U.S. Economy

Most observers seem to believe that U.S. international competitiveness is in secular decline. Press stories, speeches in international fora, and discussions with various U.S. exporters all imply a similar conclusion: that the United States has been losing trade competitiveness on a steady basis since the late 1950s. Support for this "conventional wisdom" often rests on the recent history of sizable trade and current account deficits.

My own reading of the situation leads to quite a different conclusion: that the U.S. international competitive position is quite strong today, and indeed ended the 1970s stronger than at the beginning of the decade. Let me turn to the facts that substantiate this view.

## U.S. Trade in the 1970s

The U.S. merchandise trade balance has of course deteriorated significantly over the past decade. In 1970, the merchandise trade account recorded a $3 billion surplus. At the depth of the recession in 1975, the trade surplus rose to $9 billion. While stronger than in 1978, the trade account in 1979 was in deficit by about $29 billion.

The source of this deterioration, however, is straightforward—and unrelated to the competitiveness of the United States in the world economy. The staggering increases in the cost of imported oil have not been offset by an equal increase in exports. Imported oil at the beginning of the decade cost the United States $3 billion. In 1979, the cost was $60 billion and rising rapidly.

Had we maintained the 1970 balance on all other trade, the change in the oil bill alone would have produced an overall U.S. trade deficit of $54 billion last year. Since our trade deficit was only about half that level—$29 billion to be precise—the balance on nonoil trade obviously improved. In 1970, nonoil trade was in surplus by $5 billion. At the decade's end, this surplus has risen to $31 billion. Even if we adjust for the impact of Treasury gold auctions, the surplus was about $27 billion in 1979.

The primary reason for the improvement of $20 to 25 billion was the growth in agricultural exports, which rose sharply from $7 billion in 1970 to roughly $35 billion in 1979. Many casual observers believe that the

Originally presented on July 9, 1980, before the National Foreign Trade Council in New York City.

increased value of agricultural exports resulted primarily from higher prices. In fact, the volume of U.S. agricultural exports grew strongly—almost 7 percent per annum over the decade.

Those who believe we have been losing international competitiveness would argue that the United States has a natural monopoly on much of our agricultural exports and that for authentic competition we need to look instead at trade excluding agriculture. In fact, agricultural trade is highly competitive. But if the "conventional wisdom" that we have been losing competitiveness were correct, we should expect the nonagricultural, nonoil trade balance to have deteriorated substantially during the 1970s.

This has not been the case. Our balance on nonagricultural, nonoil, trade ended the decade with only a modestly larger deficit—$5 billion—than the $2 billion deficit in 1970. This balance did deteriorate substantially in the early 1970s, before the improved U.S. competitive position that developed during the decade was reflected in our export and import performance. During 1978-1979, however, this balance strengthened sharply.

## U.S. Trade Performance

The concept of international competitiveness is easy to describe but difficult to measure statistically. I would define international competitiveness as the attractiveness, in both price and nonprice terms, of a country's export products and import substitutes compared with the goods produced in the rest of the world. No single quantitative measure is sufficient to determine a country's competitive position. Looking at an array of data, however, a general pattern for the U.S. competitive position emerges: the decade of the 1970s was a good one for U.S. international competitiveness.

The IMF publishes a series of data on international competitiveness, including five measures of price competitiveness for the thirteen key industrial countries.[1] This series is adjusted for exchange rate changes to facilitate cross-country comparisons, and it is published in a ratio form. The series measures the performance of a country against the weighted average of the other twelve. Over the decade of the 1970s the U.S. position improved on all five measures. In particular: relative U.S. export unit values improved by 12 percent; relative U.S. wholesale prices improved by 21 percent; and relative U.S. unit labor costs improved by 40 percent. In other words, the United States became more competitive. These are little recognized facts. Yet they portray important and impressive relative gains for the U.S. economy. On the basis of the same data, incidentally, Germany and Japan—usually held up as examples of superior performance—lost ground on all five measures.

These indicators suggest that the U.S. international competitive position is stronger than it was a decade ago. But improvements in competitiveness are not automatically, or even necessarily, translated into improved export performance. Competitiveness measures potential for increased exports or decreased imports. Whether or not exports in fact rise is a measure of the country's export performance.

In addition, there is a lag between changes in relative prices and resulting trade volume responses. Thus the usual performance measure for a given year reflects changes in international competitiveness in earlier years. In fact, it normally takes two or more years for a change in U.S. competitiveness to be fully realized in performance indicators such as trade flows.

The most commonly used measure of trade performance is export market shares. Most observers seem to believe that the U.S. export market share declined steadily during the 1970s and that this continued a trend begun in the late 1950s. The facts do not back up such a view.

In nominal value terms, the U.S. share of industrial country exports did in fact end the decade smaller than in 1970.[2] To get an accurate view of market shares, however, it is necessary to look at market shares in real terms. As the exports of countries whose currencies appreciated against the dollar during the period are converted from their own currencies to dollars, the statistical conversion process itself boosts the dollar value of their exports. Since the standard series on market shares is constructed in dollar terms, this in turn increases their "market shares" and reduces the U.S. share—without their exporting a single extra Volkswagon or Toyota. In short, the commonly used statistical series can give a very misleading impression of changes in the international competitive position of individual countries.

To alleviate this problem, we have constructed a series of market share data in real terms. On the basis of such volume data, U.S. market shares rose over the decade of the 1970s. Our real export market share did decline during the early 1970s, reaching a trough of 19.2 percent in 1971. But the very strong export volume growth of 1978 and 1979 resulted in a market share at the end of the decade of 20.3 percent—a full percentage point higher than the 1972 trough. This is a quite different result from that derived from the nominal data used by most observers. The attached tables show the value of U.S. exports and U.S. export shares globally and to selected markets, from 1960 through 1979 in both nominal (table 5-1) and real (table 5-2) terms.

I might add that, on the basis of this real market share data, Germany lost a full percentage point over the decade (15.9 percent in 1979 versus 16.9 percent in 1970). By contrast, Germany gained market share in nominal terms. In real terms Japan still gained substantially, increasing her share from 8.2 percent to 9.8 percent.

For the decade as a whole, the volume of total U.S. exports rose strongly.

**Table 5-1**
**U.S. Exports and Export Share (Nominal), by Major World Regions**

| | Export Value (million U.S. dollars) | | | | | | | | |
|---|---|---|---|---|---|---|---|---|---|
| *Partner* | *1960* | *1961* | *1962* | *1963* | *1964* | *1965* | *1966* | *1967* | *1968* |
| World | 20,603 | 21,034 | 21,705 | 23,374 | 26,620 | 27,509 | 30,430 | 31,603 | 34,588 |
| Developed | 13,421 | 13,770 | 14,187 | 15,313 | 17,528 | 18,615 | 20,376 | 21,693 | 23,892 |
| Communist | 519 | 303 | 369 | 440 | 483 | 341 | 520 | 502 | 496 |
| LDC | 6,663 | 6,961 | 7,149 | 7,621 | 8,609 | 8,553 | 9,534 | 9,408 | 10,200 |
| Nonoil | 4,457 | 4,695 | 4,806 | 5,268 | 5,715 | 5,745 | 6,438 | 6,367 | 6,780 |
| Oil exporters | 2,206 | 2,266 | 2,343 | 2,353 | 2,894 | 2,808 | 3,096 | 3,041 | 3,420 |
| Other | 0 | 0 | 0 | 0 | 0 | 0 | 0 | 0 | 0 |

| | Export Share (percent) | | | | | | | | |
|---|---|---|---|---|---|---|---|---|---|
| *Partner* | *1960* | *1961* | *1962* | *1963* | *1964* | *1965* | *1966* | *1967* | *1968* |
| World | 27.6 | 26.4 | 26.2 | 25.8 | 25.9 | 24.7 | 25.1 | 24.8 | 24.5 |
| Developed | 26.5 | 25.1 | 24.4 | 23.7 | 23.8 | 23.2 | 23.4 | 23.6 | 23.4 |
| Communist | 15.6 | 8.7 | 10.1 | 11.2 | 10.3 | 6.9 | 8.6 | 7.7 | 7.3 |
| LDC | 33.0 | 33.4 | 35.2 | 35.6 | 36.9 | 34.5 | 35.3 | 33.9 | 33.2 |
| Nonoil | 33.3 | 32.9 | 34.0 | 34.9 | 35.6 | 33.9 | 35.3 | 33.7 | 32.8 |
| Oil exporters | 32.4 | 34.5 | 38.0 | 37.2 | 39.9 | 35.7 | 35.2 | 34.5 | 34.1 |
| Other | 0.0 | 0.0 | 0.0 | 0.0 | 0.0 | 0.0 | 0.0 | 0.0 | 0.0 |

The total increase was 81 percent, a per annum growth rate—for all products to all markets—of 6.8 percent. Both agricultural and other exports grew at the same annual growth rate of 6.8 percent. Over the decade, world trade volume increased about 72 percent for a per annum growth rate of roughly 6.2 percent, less than the growth of U.S. exports. The data again reveal a rise in the U.S. share of world exports. [3]

Much of this U.S. gain occurred during the last two years. During 1978-1979 U.S. export volume grew 10 percent each year. World trade volumes rose at only 5.5 and 6.5 percent, respectively. Hence the United States has been increasing its market share sharply in the most recent period.

Another commonly used indicator of competitiveness is the balance of manufactures trade. The U.S. trade balance on manufactures ended the decade in a higher surplus than in 1970 ($4.4 billion in 1979, $3.4 billion in 1970). During the first five months of 1980, the surplus rose to an $8.4 billion annual rate. Again, our basic position has strengthened.

## Service Exports

Continuing growth in the surplus on services also helped strengthen the U.S. current account position during the seventies. The services sector has received little attention in most analyses of either the U.S. external position

*(Table 5-1 continued)*

| *Export Value (million U.S. Dollars)* | | | | | | | | | | |
|---|---|---|---|---|---|---|---|---|---|---|
| *1969* | *1970* | *1971* | *1972* | *1973* | *1974* | *1975* | *1976* | *1977* | *1978* | *1979* |
| 37,998 | 43,231 | 44,137 | 49,787 | 71,347 | 98,521 | 107,586 | 115,006 | 121,228 | 143,660 | 181,798 |
| 26,935 | 30,495 | 31,059 | 34,902 | 48,197 | 64,273 | 66,388 | 72,062 | 76,396 | 87,583 | 112,494 |
| 543 | 715 | 723 | 1,283 | 2,960 | 3,113 | 3,375 | 3,639 | 2,717 | 4,505 | 7,409 |
| 10,520 | 12,021 | 12,355 | 13,602 | 19,513 | 30,583 | 37,318 | 38,919 | 41,785 | 50,891 | 61,045 |
| 6,823 | 7,909 | 8,027 | 8,452 | 12,283 | 17,687 | 19,651 | 19,288 | 20,681 | 25,038 | 32,872 |
| 3,697 | 4,112 | 4,328 | 5,150 | 7,230 | 12,896 | 17,667 | 19,631 | 21,104 | 25,853 | 28,172 |
| 0 | 0 | 0 | 0 | 677 | 552 | 505 | 386 | 330 | 681 | 850 |

| *Export Share (percent)* | | | | | | | | | | |
|---|---|---|---|---|---|---|---|---|---|---|
| *1969* | *1970* | *1971* | *1972* | *1973* | *1974* | *1975* | *1976* | *1977* | *1978* | *1979* |
| 23.2 | 22.6 | 20.7 | 19.7 | 20.3 | 20.8 | 20.9 | 20.3 | 19.0 | 18.8 | 19.2 |
| 22.3 | 21.5 | 19.8 | 18.6 | 18.5 | 19.2 | 19.2 | 18.6 | 17.6 | 17.0 | 17.0 |
| 7.1 | 8.1 | 7.9 | 10.8 | 16.1 | 11.6 | 10.1 | 11.1 | 8.2 | 11.0 | 14.8 |
| 30.7 | 31.0 | 28.4 | 27.4 | 28.7 | 29.3 | 29.2 | 28.4 | 25.6 | 25.5 | 27.0 |
| 29.9 | 30.4 | 27.9 | 26.5 | 28.5 | 28.9 | 30.6 | 29.4 | 26.7 | 25.8 | 27.9 |
| 32.5 | 32.0 | 29.3 | 28.9 | 29.0 | 29.8 | 27.8 | 27.4 | 24.6 | 25.3 | 26.0 |
| 0.0 | 0.0 | 0.0 | 0.0 | 12.1 | 7.1 | 5.8 | 4.3 | 3.5 | 6.5 | 7.7 |

Source: Data are from the IMF's *Direction of Trade* and *International Financial Statistics.*

Note: Real values are calculated by dividing nominal exports by an export price index; LDC Oil Exporters are defined to be those countries that had a net surplus of crude petroleum exports in 1977. These include all the OPEC countries plus Angola, Bolivia, Brunei, Congo, Egypt, Malaysia, Mexico, Oman, Syria, Tunisia, and Zaire. "Other" includes countries not specified and "special categories." Export shares are calculated by dividing U.S. exports by exports of nineteen OECD countries: United States, Canada, Japan, Australia, Belgium/Luxembourg, Denmark, France, Ireland, Italy, Netherlands, United Kingdom, West Germany, Austria, Finland, Greece, Norway, Spain, Sweden, Switzerland.

or our basic competitiveness, but it has become a large and growing part of U.S. international activity.

As recently as 1970, gross flows in the services sector were only about $43 billion. By 1977, total U.S. trade in services had grown to $105 billion. When I spoke before the National Foreign Trade Council in November 1978, I suggested that services flows could total $140 billion in 1979. In fact, I grossly underestimated the strength of the service sector; during 1979, gross service flows totaled $175 billion. This fourfold increase in the decade kept pace with the fast growth in the value of U.S. merchandise trade.

From 1970 to 1978 the U.S. surplus on services grew from $3 billion to $25 billion. In 1979 it jumped sharply to almost $35 billion. The "invisibles" surplus after deducting private remittances and government grants of $5.5 billion, was about $29 billion,—almost wholly offsetting the merchandise trade deficit and producing near balance in our current account.

Net direct investment income accounted for almost all the improvement

**Table 5-2**
**U.S. Exports and Export Share (Real), by Major World Regions**

| | Export Value (million 1975 U.S. dollars) | | | | | | | | |
|---|---|---|---|---|---|---|---|---|---|
| *Partner* | *1960* | *1961* | *1962* | *1963* | *1964* | *1965* | *1966* | *1967* | *1968* |
| World | 44,499 | 44,564 | 46,279 | 49,944 | 56,279 | 56,371 | 60,497 | 61,604 | 66,515 |
| Developed | 28,987 | 29,174 | 30,249 | 32,720 | 37,057 | 38,145 | 40,509 | 42,287 | 45,946 |
| Communist | 1,121 | 642 | 787 | 940 | 1,021 | 699 | 1,034 | 979 | 954 |
| LDC | 14,391 | 14,748 | 15,243 | 16,284 | 18,201 | 17,527 | 18,954 | 18,339 | 19,615 |
| Nonoil | 9,626 | 9,947 | 10,247 | 11,256 | 12,082 | 11,773 | 12,799 | 12,411 | 13,038 |
| Oil exporters | 4,765 | 4,801 | 4,996 | 5,028 | 6,118 | 5,754 | 6,155 | 5,928 | 6,577 |
| Other | 0 | 0 | 0 | 0 | 0 | 0 | 0 | 0 | 0 |

| | Export Share (percent) | | | | | | | | |
|---|---|---|---|---|---|---|---|---|---|
| *Partner* | *1960* | *1961* | *1962* | *1963* | *1964* | *1965* | *1966* | *1967* | *1968* |
| World | 26.0 | 24.6 | 24.7 | 24.6 | 24.8 | 23.3 | 23.4 | 22.8 | 22.0 |
| Developed | 24.8 | 23.2 | 22.8 | 22.4 | 22.6 | 21.7 | 21.7 | 21.5 | 20.8 |
| Communist | 14.5 | 8.1 | 9.4 | 10.7 | 9.8 | 6.5 | 8.0 | 6.9 | 6.4 |
| LDC | 32.7 | 32.6 | 34.7 | 35.4 | 36.9 | 34.0 | 34.5 | 33.0 | 31.8 |
| Nonoil | 33.6 | 32.5 | 33.8 | 35.1 | 36.0 | 33.9 | 35.0 | 33.4 | 32.0 |
| Oil exporters | 31.1 | 32.9 | 36.5 | 36.1 | 38.9 | 34.3 | 33.5 | 32.4 | 31.4 |
| Other | 0.0 | 0.0 | 0.0 | 0.0 | 0.0 | 0.0 | 0.0 | 0.0 | 0.0 |

over the decade. During the seventies the surplus on direct investment income increased from a little more than $7 billion to nearly $32 billion. The level of this item was affected by a change in statistical treatment which we instituted in 1978 to conform the U.S. presentation to that of all other countries as recommended by the IMF guidelines. As a result of that change we now count reinvested earnings as an income receipt—and their reinvestment as a capital outflow. But the strong growth in this sector is unaltered by the definitional change: the surplus on remitted earnings alone rose from $4.5 billion to $17.5 billion over the decade.

## Outlook

Where is the balance going from here? Between the first quarter of 1978 and the first quarter of 1980, the nonoil, nonagricultural trade balance improved from a deficit of $7.8 billion to a small surplus of $0.3 billion. This $32 billion gain (annual rate) is impressive.

It is doubtful that our position will continue to strengthen at this pace. Nevertheless, the direction of further change seems clear at least in the short run. The U.S. recession will clearly strengthen our current account position.

*(Table 5-2 continued)*

| Export Value (million 1975 U.S. Dollars) | | | | | | | | | | |
|---|---|---|---|---|---|---|---|---|---|---|
| *1969* | *1970* | *1971* | *1972* | *1973* | *1974* | *1975* | *1976* | *1977* | *1978* | *1979* |
| 70,760 | 76,245 | 75,319 | 82,566 | 101,345 | 110,202 | 107,586 | 111,010 | 112,561 | 124,705 | 134,965 |
| 50,158 | 53,783 | 53,002 | 57,881 | 68,462 | 71,894 | 66,388 | 69,558 | 70,934 | 76,027 | 83,515 |
| 1,011 | 1,261 | 1,234 | 2,128 | 4,205 | 3,482 | 3,375 | 3,513 | 2,522 | 3,910 | 5,501 |
| 19,590 | 21,201 | 21,084 | 22,557 | 27,717 | 34,209 | 37,318 | 37,567 | 38,798 | 44,176 | 45,319 |
| 12,706 | 13,949 | 13,698 | 14,017 | 17,447 | 19,784 | 19,651 | 18,618 | 19,203 | 21,734 | 24,404 |
| 6,885 | 7,252 | 7,386 | 8,541 | 10,270 | 14,425 | 17,667 | 18,949 | 19,595 | 22,442 | 20,915 |
| 0 | 0 | 0 | 0 | 962 | 617 | 505 | 373 | 306 | 591 | 631 |

| Export Share (percent) | | | | | | | | | | |
|---|---|---|---|---|---|---|---|---|---|---|
| *1969* | *1970* | *1971* | *1972* | *1973* | *1974* | *1975* | *1976* | *1977* | *1978* | *1979* |
| 20.7 | 20.5 | 19.2 | 19.3 | 20.6 | 20.7 | 20.9 | 19.7 | 19.1 | 20.1 | 20.3 |
| 19.8 | 19.3 | 18.1 | 18.1 | 18.7 | 19.0 | 19.2 | 18.0 | 17.8 | 18.2 | 18.1 |
| 6.2 | 7.2 | 7.2 | 10.6 | 16.4 | 11.6 | 10.1 | 10.7 | 8.2 | 11.8 | 15.5 |
| 29.4 | 30.0 | 28.0 | 28.7 | 31.1 | 30.9 | 30.2 | 28.5 | 26.6 | 28.4 | 29.6 |
| 29.2 | 30.1 | 28.1 | 28.5 | 32.0 | 31.6 | 32.8 | 30.8 | 28.8 | 30.0 | 31.8 |
| 29.9 | 29.7 | 27.7 | 28.9 | 29.7 | 30.0 | 27.8 | 26.5 | 24.8 | 27.0 | 27.3 |
| 0.0 | 0.0 | 0.0 | 0.0 | 12.5 | 7.4 | 5.8 | 4.2 | 3.5 | 6.8 | 7.8 |

Source: Data are from the IMF's *Direction of Trade* and *International Financial Statistics.*

Note: Real values are calculated by dividing nominal exports by an export price index; LDC Oil Exporters are defined to be those countries that had a net surplus of crude petroleum exports in 1977. These include all the OPEC countries plus Angola, Bolivia, Brunei, Congo, Egypt, Malaysia, Mexico, Oman, Syria, Tunisia, and Zaire. "Other" includes countries not specified and "special categories." Export shares are calculated by dividing U.S. exports by exports of nineteen OECD countries: United States, Canada, Japan, Australia, Belgium/Luxembourg, Denmark, France, Ireland, Italy, Netherlands, United Kingdom, West Germany, Austria, Finland, Greece, Norway, Spain, Sweden, Switzerland.

From March through May, as the recession hit, our current account returned to rough balance as exports continued to grow and imports (including oil imports) dropped sharply.

Perhaps as important, from a longer-term perspective, has been the slowing of oil imports. Higher prices to consumers are obviously reducing demand. During the first five months of this year, oil imports were running 12 percent below the same period last year. At today's prices, this represents a saving of over $10 billion on imported oil. I believe that we will continue to see declines in the volume of oil imports.

Aside from price competitiveness, which I have already addressed, the other basic determination of trade flows is income growth. The U.S. trade balance is affected strongly by relative growth rates at home and abroad. Improvements in the U.S. trade balance or current account would provide little cause for optimism if they derived solely, or even importantly, from a slowdown in our own economy. In an effort to gain a better understanding of the underlying trade and current balances, we have therefore attempted to look at cyclically adjusted positions as well.

This is a very tricky area, and the results can be taken only as rough orders of magnitude. But the range of available estimates suggests that the United States was operating *closer* to full employment in 1979 than were our major trading partners. Had all major trading countries been operating at something like full capacity, the underlying U.S. trade balance would therefore have been considerably stronger. Our imports might have been $7-10 billion higher, but our nonagricultural exports would have been $15-20 billion larger. Thus our cyclically adjusted trade deficit in 1979 might have been around $20 billion rather than the $29 billion deficit actually recorded. Our current account would have been in sizable surplus.

Hence cyclical factors do not obviate the encouraging recent trends in the U.S. external position. It is impossible to put forth precise numbers, but it seems that the U.S. current account will be at least in rough balance for the three-year period from 1979 to 1981, which is about as far ahead as anyone can hope to see. The year 1979 was virtually in balance. We had a sizable deficit in the first quarter of 1980 as the big OPEC price increase passed into the import statistics, but we subsequently saw a return to rough balance. Our latest estimates suggest an even stronger picture into 1981. The three-year picture appears to be, at a minimum, one of rough equilibrium.

## Conclusion

I have presented a relatively optimistic view of both U.S. international competitiveness and the outlook for our current account. From a policy standpoint, however, we clearly cannot rest on past achievements. Exports are an essential and growing element of the U.S. economy, generating substantial employment and production at home. Export expansion provides the only appropriate means of paying for the increased cost of needed imports, including oil. With economic growth slowing throughout the world, the competition for export markets will be fierce.

Hence the United States must compete even more effectively in world markets in the future. Strong efforts will be needed by both U.S. industry and the U.S. Government to take full advantage of the strong underlying competitive position which I have described today—and to improve it further in the future.

We can do so, however, on the basis of a U.S. export performance over the past decade that has been considerably stronger than most observers recognize. The fundamental competitive position of the United States has improved. There is no reason to believe that U.S. exports are less attractive than those of other countries. Given the appropriate stimulus and support, our export performance can be improved further—thereby helping to meet a number of cardinal economic objectives of the United States for the foreseeable future.

## Notes

1. The series are relative unit labor costs, relative normalized unit labor costs, relative value-added deflators, relative wholesale prices, and relative export unit values.

2. It should be noted that developing countries seized a growing share of world exports of manufactured goods during the 1970s, reducing the share of industrial countries as a group and of most individual industrial countries. Unfortunately, there exist no consistent data series which permit a systematic evaluation of their importance. Lags in data detail and absence of consistent price deflators also delay timely analysis; we therefore use throughout the standard series of export data for the nineteen major OECD countries.

3. This is a different, broader calculation than used in the preceding paragraphs, which was linked to shares of developed country exports only.

# 6 The International Arrangement on Export Credits

The long-standing goal of U.S. efforts in the field of international arrangements on export credits has been to reduce and eliminate subsidies. These subsidies are not small. Mr. Axel Wallen, the Chairman of the Organization for Economic Cooperation and Development's Export Credits Group, has estimated that the industrialized OECD countries participating in the Arrangement on Guidelines for Officially Supported Export Credits may provide between $3 and $5 billion dollars in export credit subsidies this year.

To achieve our goals, we have developed and implemented a two-track strategy. The first track is intensive negotiations to limit subsidies multilaterally. The second track is a more aggressive Eximbank, to indicate clearly that the United States will not permit its exporters to be rendered uncompetitive as a result of the export credit practices of other countries.

## The First Track—International Negotiations

On the first track, we have pressed increasingly hard for meaningful international negotiations. In the past three years alone, we have had 31 bilateral and multilateral talks with Arrangement participants. These negotiations have been even more intense than the celebrated Subsidy Code talks in the Multilateral Trade Negotiations. Let me summarize the progress we have made in the export credits arena since 1975.

At the Rambouillet Summit in 1975, the general principles of a Consensus on Export Credits were laid down. That Consensus provided for the beginning of discipline in the export credit area by establishing minimum interest rates and maximum maturity terms. This first step was followed by a second at the London Summit of 1977. The London Summit provided the impetus for an International Arrangement on Guidelines for Officially Supported Export Credits, a more formal understanding, which came into force in April 1978. In October 1978, we began pressing for further improvements in the Arrangement, most of which were not accepted at that time by our trading partners.

Originally presented on June 12, 1980, before the Subcommittee on International Trade, Investment and Monetary Policy of the U.S. Committee on Banking, Finance and Urban Affairs.

In March 1979, President Carter reported to Congress on the state of the negotiations to improve the Arrangement. He noted that the unanimity required to increase the Arrangement interest rate structure was lacking, and that, as a result, we would modify Eximbank's programs to be more aggressive. The President added that we would press ahead with negotiations when other countries showed more willingness to achieve a greater measure of international discipline.

Last fall, other countries showed a willingness to try again and a new round of negotiations began. The most important result so far is the Wallen Report, named after its principal author. The report proposed an entirely new framework for official export credits.

## The New Framework

There are two basic problems with the existing Arrangement. First, it specifies minimum interest rates which any export credit agency can offer to foreign borrowers. These rates have remained unchanged since July 1, 1976. Fluctuations in market interest rates, particularly in an upward direction, have thus produced sharp divergences between the Arrangement minima and the level of interest rates in a given capital market. This generates major increases in official export credit subsidy levels.

Second, the Arrangement's interest rates are identical for all currencies: the Arrangement minima apply whether the credit is in U.S. dollars, Swiss francs, or some other currency. However, market rates differ sharply from country to country (as well as over time, for all countries). Pronounced anomalies can thus appear among countries, with major competitive implications.

The new framework proposed in the Wallen Report involves a differentiated rate system for export credits, which would rectify both problems. It would vary the minimum interest rates on official export credits by currency, and it would synchronize these minimum interest rates with actual rates in the respective capital markets.

The idea would be to have a different interest rate minimum for each lending currency. The market rates of interest on loans in the currency of a country with a low rate of inflation tend to be lower than for loans in the currency of a country with a high rate of inflation. Given that the minimum rates of interest are the same for all currencies under the present Arrangement on Export Credits, a high-inflation-rate country can subsidize exports as compared to a low-inflation-rate country and still comply with the Arrangement interest rate minima. The new framework would eliminate this competitive inequity.

Second, the proposed new framework would not only relate the minimum interest rates to market rates of interest in the various major currencies, it would change these rates from time to time as capital market rates change. The idea would be to adjust the minimum interest rates, periodically and automatically, using long-term government bond yields in the various countries as benchmarks. This would avoid the built-in delays we face at present in trying to adjust Arrangement interest rates by negotiation.

The U.S. Government firmly supports a differentiated rate system. Such a system would place all official export credit offers on a much more equitable basis. It would greatly reduce subsidies and the dangers of an export credit war.

## An Interim Measure

In mid-May of this year, the Participants in the Arrangement, some twenty-two industrial nations, met in Paris to consider the Wallen proposals. At the meeting, the European Economic Community (EEC) announced that it was not yet ready to approve a differentiated rate system along the lines proposed in the Wallen Report. The Europeans did offer, without prejudice to further consideration of the Wallen proposals, to raise the present Arrangement minimum interest rates by ¼ percent for loans to poor countries and ¾ percent for the intermediate and rich countries. This will take effect July 1st and is a step in the right direction. It will reduce the subsidy by participants on export credits this year by as much as several hundred million dollars.

By itself, the EEC offer was clearly inadequate. But it was acceptable as an interim measure. At the Paris meeting, it was agreed that December 1, 1980 would be the deadline for reaching agreements on a revision of the Arrangement.

I followed up on the start made at the May meeting in Paris by urging strong support from ministers of economy and finance at the OECD ministerial meeting last week. The ministers agreed to support fully efforts to adapt the terms of the International Arrangement on Export Credits, bringing them closer in line with current market conditions. While welcoming the immediate adjustment of minimum interest rates, the ministers encouraged the Arrangement participants to reach a mutually acceptable overall solution by December 1st.

President Carter will raise this issue at the Venice Summit later this month. That will be the litmus test of whether there is sufficient political will to reduce export credit subsidies. And it does require political will by our major trading partners.

**Interest Rate Illusion**

An accepted revision will not be easily accomplished because some participants in the Arrangement claim that currencies permitted to charge lower interest rates than others would be favored by importers. Such borrower behavior is called "interest rate illusion." Buyers infected with this illusion are said to be concerned only with the nominal interest rate of a loan and not with the currency in which it is denominated. The supposed rationale for the illusion is that future exchange rates are unpredictable, and hence are disregarded by borrowers.

No one can predict with confidence what future exchange rates will be, but the existence of interest rate illusion is supported neither by experience nor by theory. Buyers ordinarily do have some exchange rate expectations in mind when considering competing export credit offers. Indeed, expected exchange rate movements are generally reflected in interest rate differentials. Nonetheless, those exporting nations that believe in the existence of interest rate illusion prefer the present Arrangement—with one rate for all currencies—to a differentiated rate system.

The practical answer to the proponents of interest rate illusion is that, under a differentiated rate system, all official export credit agencies would be able to offer export credits in any currency. If a buyer prefers lower interest credits in a foreign hard currency, then the official export agency could offer such credits. In fact, Eximbank has already taken the step of guaranteeing loans in foreign currencies. Should a differentiated rate system be adopted by the Arrangement participants, we would be ready to consider having Eximbank denominate direct credits in foreign currencies.

**A More Aggressive Eximbank—The Second Track**

While we have sought through negotiations to reduce export credit subsidies, we have also supported this effort by creating a more aggressive direct lending program at Eximbank. Our pace on this second track has been evident to both U.S. exporters and our foreign trading partners.

In fiscal 1977 Eximbank's direct loan program amounted to $700 million. In fiscal 1978, it jumped to $2.9 billion. We increased this to $3.7 billion in fiscal 1979. In fiscal 1980, the Administration went further still, and proposed a $5.1 billion Eximbank, $4.1 billion in direct budget funds and $1 billion on a standby basis from the Federal Financing Bank (FFB). For fiscal 1981, the Administration requested $4.4 billion in direct loan funds and another $1 billion FFB Standby.

The Bank has made aggressive use of the substantial resources this administration has commited to it. In 1979, the Bank began to match, on a selective basis, the type of predatory financing addressed in Congressman Leach's bill (H.R. 6596). Eximbank offered $100 million to Tunisia at an interest rate of 5.5 percent to match the mixed credit offers of other countries. The Bank also matched foreign mixed credit competition twice in Cyprus and won. It has done this as well in Greece.

In addition to matching specific mixed credits, the Bank has matched foreign official credit competition generally. To be fully competitive, it has reduced its interest rates and increased its participation in export transactions. For example, the average Eximbank "cover" before the newly aggressive stance was approximately 40 percent. Now, it is over 55 percent. On nonaircraft cases, the "cover" is over 70 percent. The Bank's average interest rate on this increased cover has remained at an average of about 8.3 percent despite rising market rates of interest, in order to match foreign official credit competition.

The Bank's program of increased cover and relatively low interest rates has helped make U.S. exporters much more competitive when faced with officially supported finance from foreign sources. Combined with more basic economic factors, this has helped produce a substantial growth in U.S. exports.

The volume of U.S. nonagricultural exports (excluding gold) did not grow at all from 1975 through 1977. But in 1978 such exports rose 8.2 percent by volume, and in 1979 the increase was 15.2 percent by volume and over 27 percent by value—more than twice the growth of world trade. The bottom line of our export expansion effort has thus been quite positive. Nevertheless, we must continue to press our trading partners to agree to reduce subsidies on export credits, and continue to have a strong Export-Import Bank to match those trading partners who are recalcitrant in these negotiations.

**Next Steps in the Negotiations**

The next six months will be the critical period of the negotiations. We must overcome the considerable objections that other countries have to adopting a differentiated rate system. No one should be under the illusion that all other countries are yet ready to accept a market-oriented approach to official export credit finance.

As I described earlier, some countries object to a system of differentiated interest rates on the ground that "interest rate illusion" rules borrower behavior.

In addition, some countries object to reducing interest rate subsidies on export credits to developing nations because of North-South implications. Others use the North-South argument as an excuse to subsidize exports for mercantilistic reasons. Still other countries use subsidized export credits to meet domestic adjustment problems. Yet others wish to keep their rates low for reasons of monetary prestige.

Since these objections and our answers to them are the crux of the negotiations, I would like to explain them in some detail.

## Export Credits as Aid

A few countries are beginning to view official export credits as a means of transferring resources to the less developed countries (LDCs), which are the principal borrowers. They argue that raising export credit interest rates would crimp the flow of resources to the LDCs. Subsidized resource transfers may seem especially necessary when most LDCs have been hit hard by oil import needs and are consequently experiencing balance-of-payments problems.

There are several responses to this line of argument. First, an export credit program should be viewed as a commercial program designed to facilitate exports through assumption by the government of various credit risks private creditors are unwilling to take. Export credit programs should not be seen as a substitute for genuine aid. If countries wish to increase the aid they give LDCs, they should do it through programs that directly benefit the LDCs rather than their own exporters.

Second, the main beneficiaries of official export credits are the richer LDCs, such as Korea and Mexico, and the intermediate category countries such as the nations of Eastern Europe. These nations do not require aid nearly as much as countries that have low per capita incomes, if they need it at all.

Third, the sectors that benefit from official export credits are not necessarily the ones that most benefit the poorest segments of an LDC economy. The exports tend to be capital-intensive manufactured goods, while the truly poor people need help in more basic areas such as agriculture.

Finally, the World Bank, the regional development banks, the International Monetary Fund, and bilateral assistance agencies are far more efficient and effective in addressing development and balance of payments problems than are official export credit agencies. The purposes of the two sets of agencies should not be confused.

## Mixed Credits

A subset of the development assistance argument is the contention that mixed credits help stretch economic development funds. Mixed credits, as you know, are a combination of foreign aid and official export credits yielding an overall cost to the borrower less than the Arrangement minimum.

We have sought to counter this practice by selectively matching egregious examples of mixed credits. While we would normally not choose the least developed countries for matching, we see no justification at all for mixed credits in the more economically advanced countries. Therefore, with a view toward competing with, rather than supplementing mixed credits by others, we are matching in such countries as Tunisia, Cyprus, and Greece.

We intend to continue the selective matching of foreign mixed credits until we achieve real progress in reducing their use. This issue has been frequently discussed at various bilateral and multilateral meetings and we believe that there is sufficient international concern that improvements also will be forthcoming in this area.

### Mercantilism

Another basis for export credit subsidies is, in essence, modern mercantilism. As we have reduced import barriers, some countries have invented less visible beggar-thy-neighbor policies.

These mercantilistic countries have used official export credits as a tool to support troubled domestic industries and to promote their exports. Some national export credit programs are run on the basis that virtually every exporter is entitled to subsidized credits. As a result, official export credit competition is one of the major trade issues remaining from the Multilateral Trade Negotiations.

The rebuttal to the mercantilist argument is straightforward: export credit subsidies work only if no other country is willing to match them. Over the last few years, it has become clear that export credit agencies are willing to match each others' programs. Because Eximbank has been aggressively matching competing subsidy offers, its export financing activities have grown. For example, Eximbank had larger long-term direct credit programs in 1978 than Japan, the United Kingdom, France, or Germany.

In addition to this practical reason for avoiding export credit subsidies, there is another. The major trading countries agreed to restrict direct export subsidies in the Multilateral Trade Negotiations. We hope that we can impress upon other countries the illogic of restricting subsidy practices in one area but expanding them in another. Such practices run absolutely contrary to the efforts of industrial nations to facilitate the adjustment of their industries to changing world market conditions. While all governments assist selected industries from time to time, a program that entitles all industries to export subsidies contradicts both the basic concepts of positive adjustment and open trading relationships.

### Future Steps

As already noted, the second half of 1980 will be the critical period for the negotiations on the Arrangements. The next step is discussion at the Venice Summit. The President is determined at the Summit to press these negotiations to a successful conclusion.

We seek from the Venice Summit a clear directive that will support the reforms we have been urging over the past three years. Without this high-level directive, our efforts to negotiate an improvement in the Arrangement are likely to become bogged in a morass of petty objections and technical differences.

While we hope that a satisfactory improvement in the Arrangement can be negotiated, we do not intend to ignore the possibility that it may not be. If there is no progress in the next six months, we must consider the following steps in addition to those taken during the past three years to make the Eximbank more competitive:

1. In specific cases, we might have to begin extending maturities if the budgetary cost of matching subsidized foreign interest rates proves too high. We could, for example, offer terms of fifteen years for aircraft, or twenty or thirty years for power plants.

2. Where countries have export subsidy programs which are particularly nettlesome to us, we would respond on a case-by-case basis in a manner designed to discomfort them to the maximum extent possible.

3. We would seek to enlarge the financial guarantee program, and make it more attractive to investors, so that it can relieve pressure on the direct loan budget. In this regard, we would seek to involve insurance companies, pension funds, and other long-term investors in export finance, an investment possibility they have not developed fully.

4. We would expand our efforts to establish common lines on financing particular kinds of transactions with countries sympathetic to our point of view. Even now there is a "best endeavors" clause in the International Arrangement which encourages such efforts. In more than one instance we have been able to achieve informal agreement, demonstrating that reduced export credit subsidization is possible.

### Federal Financing Bank

In addition to these steps, we need more direct loan capability for Eximbank. As you know, the Bank is operating under a Continuing Resolution. As a result, this may be the first time in history that Eximbank will run out of lending authority before the end of its fiscal year. It goes without saying that in order to continue to meet aggressive export credit competition from foreign governments, the United States needs a strong and fully competitive Eximbank—certainly not one which is practically out of funds for fiscal 1980 and already precommitted for direct loans to the extent of $2.1 billion in fiscal 1981.

There is a way of getting us through fiscal year 1980 and taking care of many of the problems being created by deferrals to fiscal 1981. That is to resort to Federal Financing Bank (FFB) Standby funding for Eximbank to the extent of $1 billion in each of the two years fiscal 1980 and fiscal 1981.

We are sympathetic to the concerns of the Congress about backdoor financing. But this is not backdoor financing. The Congress has full budgetary oversight, in that the administration's budget requests $250 million in guarantee authority to cover the prospective $1 billion FFB Standby in fiscal 1980, with a similar request made for fiscal 1981.

Eximbank's guarantees are limited by Congress in an appropriation bill through the limitation on Eximbank's Program Activity. The administration does not intend to initiate this program without full consultation with the leaders of the appropriate congressional committees.

To accommodate the proposed $4.1 billion fiscal 1980 direct loan budget figure, and $1 billion in FFB Standby funds, we would increase the Continuing Resolution Program Limit from $5,347,300,000 to $5,947,300,000, an increase of $600 million—of which $350 million would be due to the increase in the direct loan portion from $3.75 billion to $4.1 billion, and the balance, $250 million, to the Eximbank guarantees necessary to support the $1 billion of FFB Standby funds.

The FFB Standby has several advantages as a means of increasing Eximbank resources. First, it costs only 25 cents on the dollar against the fiscal 1980 budget authorization ceiling. In this respect, it has the same impact on the federal budget as does Eximbank-guaranteed money provided by the Private Funding Corporation.

Second, it does not entail budget outlays as the obligor would be a foreign borrower, even though the loan would be fully guaranteed by Eximbank.

Third, an FFB loan guaranteed by Eximbank entails the least expense to the U.S. government of any guarantee alternative. It is, for example, much less costly than subsidizing private bank loans.

The FFB Standby arrangement can act as a safety valve for Eximbank. Using it for large transactions will free an equivalent amount of direct credits for other exports. In a period of tight budget stringency, which we clearly face at present, the FFB Standby appears to be a particularly attractive vehicle to promote our dual purposes of (1) assuring a fully competitive Eximbank and (2) thereby strengthening our position in negotiations to improve the International Arrangement.

## How the FFB Standby Would Operate

Under the administration's FFB Standby proposal, foreign borrowers would go through the Eximbank approval process just as they do now. The Eximbank Board would decide what interest rate to offer the borrower in view of competing foreign offers. The borrower would then go to the FFB to receive his financing, while Eximbank would guarantee repayment to the FFB. Under this arrangement, the FFB loan would be covered by the Eximbank guarantees and insurance budget.

The FFB charges the same interest rate to all its users, 12.5 basis points over its cost of money when it issues Treasury securities of maturity equivalent to the borrowing involved. If the interest rate Eximbank fixes to the borrower is less than the FFB rate, Eximbank would absorb the difference just as it does now. As you know, all Eximbank direct loan funding is through the FFB.

## Pending Legislation

The administration appreciates that the two bills under consideration by this committee are intended to improve the competitive position of U.S. exporters. The Leach bill—HR 6596—calls for Eximbank to offer programs comparable to those offered by our principal competitors. The intent of the bill is to reduce and ultimately eliminate export credit subsidies.

The administration supports the intent of the bill. We may need it at some point in the future. But for now, we believe the $1 billion of increased credit availability from the Federal Financing Bank on a standby basis is sufficient for providing Eximbank the necessary financial resources to match foreign official credit competition.

The second bill under consideration—H.R. 6595—would establish firm criteria for the Export Expansion Facility. We welcome this expression of congressional intent. But we are fearful that expanded use of this facility may result in high-risk lending and losses which would further strain the Bank's net income position, during a period when it is already under pressure from matching foreign competition. Moreover, earmarking further funds for the EEF will not, by itself, increase the total pool of resources available to the Bank.

## Conclusion

While several bills have been introduced which would give Eximbank additional flexibility to combat predatory practices of other governments, the

Bank's most critical need at the moment is to have the funding necessary for the rest of this fiscal year. Accordingly, Eximbank and the administration propose for fiscal 1980 that Eximbank's direct credit authority be increased from the $3.75 billion Continuing Resolution level under which it is presently operating, to $4.1 billion, and that an additional $1 billion for export credits be made available through an FFB Standby guaranteed by Eximbank (requiring an increase in Eximbank's current guarantee budget).

The administration will continue to support a strong and fully competitive Eximbank. We will continue to seek improvements in the International Arrangement on Export Credits, to reduce and eventually eliminate the subsidy element in export credits, building on the modest but meaningful progress achieved over the last four weeks.

# 7 The Export Credit Policy of the United States: Meeting International Competition Effectively

The strength of U.S. exports during the 1980s will be critical to the ability of our nation to pay for imports of oil and other commodities, to maintain the stability of the dollar in the exchange markets, and to achieve key economic policy objectives such as reasonably full employment. Indeed, exports are increasingly important to our economy because one of every seven U.S. manufacturing jobs and 1 of every 3 acres of U.S. farmland now produce for export; $1 of every $3 of U.S. corporate profit now derives from the international activities of U.S. firms, including their investments overseas as well as exports; and the share of exports in U.S. gross national product (GNP) has doubled within just the last decade.

It is therefore extremely fortunate that, contrary to the views expressed by some observers, the underlying competitive position of the U.S. economy has been improving substantially. The increase of $40 billion in the U.S. oil import bill since 1977 has obscured the fact that the rest of our trade balance has improved by an even greater amount, largely because exports have been doing very well.

> During the past three years the volume of U.S. nonagricultural exports has grown at a rate double that of world trade, producing a sharp rise in U.S. market shares.
>
> The United States alone accounted for one-third of the increased volume of industrial nations' exports during 1978 and 1979, with the growth occurring across all industry sectors and most geographic markets.
>
> The U.S. volume share of industrial nations' exports (excluding exports to the United States) now exceeds 21 percent, higher than at any other time during the past decade.
>
> In value terms, U.S. exports have doubled since 1976.

---

Originally presented on December 8, 1980, before the Annual Bankers Conference of the Export-Import Bank in Washington, D.C.

> Our trade surplus on manufactured goods was running at an annual rate of $18.2 billion during the first 10 months of 1980, up from $4.4 billion in 1979 and $3.4 billion in 1970.
>
> Largely as a result, the U.S. current account moved into balance in 1979 and will almost certainly remain there, or even in modest surplus, in 1980-1981. This gives us the strongest external position in the entire OECD area, and underpins the rise of almost 10 percent in the trade-weighted exchange rate of the dollar over the past two years.

The Export-Import Bank has played an important role in this success story, by again providing export finance of a level and nature that support the competitive postition of American industry:

> Its direct export loans have increased sevenfold during the past four years.
>
> It has maintained competitive interest rates in the face of substantial increases in borrowing costs within the U.S. market, and thus important costs to its own financial position.
>
> It has taken other measures where necessary to match foreign competition.

These instances of real progress, however, are no basis for complacency. To the contrary, the United States will have to run hard even to maintain the gains of the recent past. We will need to do even better in the highly competitive world economy of the 1980s.

In fact, we now stand at a crossroads in terms of supporting the U.S. competitive position in international markets. A key measure employed by other nations to increase their exports is the use of subsidized export credits. For the past four years, the United States has actively pursued a two-track strategy to counter such policies. On the one hand, we already noted, we have sharply increased both the quantity and quality of support provided to U.S. exporters by our own Eximbank.

On the other hand, we have sought to negotiate international restraints on the subsidy element in official export credits. We have had some success in establishing minimum interest rates and in obtaining prior notification of the credit terms other official export credit agencies are offering in nearly all instances—which is highly valuable information as it provides Eximbank the knowledge of what it should match.

The level of interest rates is now far too low relative to actual market rates. The inherent subsidy due to differences in the cost of funds to governments (now exceeding $5 billion for the OECD countries, taken together) is threatening to create a mutually disruptive export credit war.

Despite this real danger, the European Community has been willing only to suggest the adoption of marginal increases in the interest rate minima. This would leave a larger gap between export credit rates and market rates than existed last July when the heads of government at the Venice Summit committed their countries to move closer to market rates. We hope that the European Community will change its mind and join the rest of the world in recognizing the serious need to reduce disruptive interest rate subsidization in the provision of export credits.

In the absence of a negotiated solution to this problem, we are fully prepared—as already announced—to derogate from the present International Arrangement, as necessary, to stand behind U.S. exporters facing such foreign official competition. I would like to comment on our export credit policy and consider where it is going over the months and years ahead.

## The International Arrangement on Official Export Credits

The U.S. government has led the way in seeking to avoid the costly foolishness of an export credit war. In July 1976, it induced the major trading countries—Canada, France, Germany, Italy, Japan, and the United Kingdom—to agree to reduce the risks of an export credit war by adopting consensus guidelines designed to reduce subsidies in government-supported export credits. That consensus was subsequently adopted by other member countries of the Organization for Economic Cooperation and Development. It included two basic components: minimum levels beneath which interest rates on official export credits should not be offered, and maximum maturities beyond which such credits should not extend. Given the structural superiority of U.S. capital markets in generating long-term capital, the basic agreement was that the United States would limit its maturities if the other countries would limit their interest rate subsidies.

In 1977-1978, the United States sought to improve the consensus via an increase in minimum interest rates and other improvements. However, the only progress made at that time was to convert the original understanding into the present, more formal, International Arrangement on Official Export Credits. The major weakness of this Arrangement has been that its minimum interest rates have not reflected market rates of interest for the different currencies of the exporting nations. It also fails to cover such undesirable practices as mixed credits and excessive local cost financing, but we have set those aside from the negotiations for the moment—while responding to them ourselves on a case-by-case basis—in an effort to deal first with the more fundamental aspects of the Arrangement.

Since 1978, there has been increasing international recognition of the need to provide more discipline in export credit financing. At the end of

1979, the OECD-sponsored "Wallen Report" estimated that the level of export credit subsidization had risen to $2 billion in 1978 and $5 billion in 1979. To remedy the situation, the Report spelled out ways to reduce the subsidies without placing any country at a disadvantage. It offered two alternatives to accomplish this objective: a differentiated rate system (DRS) and a moving uniform matrix system (MUM).

The United States preferred the differentiated rate system, which would set different interest rate minimums for each of the different exporter currencies. It would thus most closely approximate market conditions. Other countries were less willing to accept a differentiated rate system, however. As a compromise, the United States indicated that the other alternative offered by the Wallen Report, the moving uniform matrix, would also be acceptable. This would involve a weighted average of interest rates in the participating countries that would determine the new export credit minimum rate for all countries. This miminum rate would change as market rates changed, ideally automatically. And it would clearly represent a marked improvement over the present system. We would also permit low-interest-rate countries to opt for the DRS.

Negotiations on this issue initially came to a head last summer. At that time, in lieu of the basic reform proposed in the Wallen Report, the European Community proposed a modest increase in minimum interest rates, to be followed by intensive negotiations aimed at bringing interest rates closer to market conditions. The United States reluctantly accepted this temporizing, but indicated quite clearly—both privately and publicly—that we would have to derogate from the Arrangement ourselves if fundamental improvements were not agreed to soon. At the Venice Summit in July, the major members of the European Community then agreed with the other participants that the negotiations should bring export credit rates closer to market rates. These negotiations were to be concluded by December 1, 1980.

The commitments of the Venice Summit have not been met. The European Community (EC) has again offered only to increase interest rates by a minimal amount (along with a vague reference to further discussions throughout 1981 on broader reform of the export credit rate system). The increase in interest rates offered by the European Community would bring the minimum interest rate for credits to the major users of such facilities only to 8.35 percent. Under the moving uniform matrix, the minimum interest rate would be at least 10.5 to 11 percent, much closer to most financial market rates. Indeed, under the EC proposal, Arrangement minimum rates would be farther from market rates than they were when the heads of state at the Summit committed to close the gap last July.

It is unconscionable, as well as deeply disappointing, that such a minority can thwart the efforts of a vast majority of the international community to achieve needed restraint in this key trade area. In response, the United

States has announced its intention to derogate, on a selective basis, from the terms of the International Arrangement and to extend credits with 15- to 20-year (or longer) maturities, as a means of meeting foreign export credit interest rate subsidies. If the interest rate component of the basic deal on export credits—not to mention the Summit commitment—cannot be kept by others, it will be impossible for the United States to keep the maturity component of the deal.

Moreover, key Republican members of the U.S. Senate—Senators Garn and Heinz, who between them will shortly become chairmen of the key committees in the Senate regarding this issue—have publicly indicated their strong support for our efforts to make clear that they are being pursued on a bipartisan basis. The Senate's recent addition of $1 billion of Exim funding to the Continuing Resolution is of course not unrelated.

The United States remains ready to negotiate a meaningful reform of the International Arrangement. We appreciate the support for our efforts displayed by almost every country involved in these negotiations. We do not intend to direct our weapon of longer repayment maturities against those countries which offer realistic export credit rates. But we are determined to assure competitive financing for U.S. exports. We prefer to do so by raising export credit interest rates toward market levels in all countries, and we will continue to negotiate to that end.

## The Program of the Export-Import Bank

During the past year, Eximbank has been able to offer export credits at competitive rates only by drawing from its longer-term earnings stream. In fact, the Bank has been lending at rates far below its marginal cost of money—and, lately, even below its average costs. It can no longer provide such subsidies and hope to be self-sufficient. If it does, we expect the Bank to be in the red for the coming fiscal years as a result of the necessity to maintain aggressive lending practices and the likelihood of continuing high borrowing costs. This could greatly hamper the Bank in supporting U.S. exports. Similar situations of course obtain in most other countries as well, indicating why it is so urgent to buttress fundamentally the International Arrangement.

From our standpoint, the longer repayment terms offered under derogations from the Arrangement will enable the Bank to charge interest rates more in line with market conditions. Thus they will be very helpful in strengthening the Bank's ability to remain self-sufficient.

At the same time, however, this action may not be enough to fully support U.S. exports on competitive financial terms. The administration is therefore examining other ways to assure sufficient as well as competitive

Eximbank financing. This is a critical problem. To meet foreign competition, the Bank has offered heavily subsidized rates. These rates have eroded the financial health of the Bank. To restore that health, we must consider innovative measures to keep Eximbank functioning in support of U.S. exports.

My personal preference for a solution, and one that the new administration should consider, is the creation of a special fund—perhaps within Treasury, similar to those of France and the United Kingdom—to subsidize interest rates on particular Eximbank loans. Such a fund would permit Eximbank itself to carry out the bulk of its borrowing and lending operations without subsidy, enabling it to meet most foreign credit competition without endangering its financial self-sufficiency—and justifying its removal from the current process of seeking annual budget for the U.S. government.

The subsidy fund could be established with a sunset provision to assure that the United States does not remain permanently in the business of subsidizing export credits, keyed inter alia to restoration of an effective International Arrangement limiting subsidies for all countries. The U.S. government, via Eximbank, would offer interest rate subsidies from the new fund only as necessary to meet foreign competition.

## Conclusion

The area of export credits provides a clear example of the increasing tendency of foreign governments to seek to tilt the benefits of international commerce in their direction through the use of beggar-thy-neighbor policies. Indeed, the central strategic issue for U.S. economic policy in the 1980s will be whether we should fight or join this trend.

Our clear preference—and our traditional instinct—has been to negotiate common rules for the international marketplace to assure fair competition for all parties and to try to limit government intervention in the process. We now have an international code governing the use of most export subsidies, as a result of the recent Multilateral Trade Negotiations. In fact, the major trade policy issue left unresolved at the conclusion of those negotiations was export credits.

Until we can achieve more effective rules governing export finance, however, and as long as some others refuse to compete fairly, we will have to counter with equivalent policies of our own. We have made every effort to achieve a negotiated solution, and we will continue to do so. We have not yet succeeded adequately, however, and we have therefore begun to counter with measures of our own. We can go much further, if necessary, and we may have to do so, given the importance of exports to U.S. domestic and international economic policy.

This issue may prove to be the exception to traditional U.S. practice: we may have to join the trend toward increased government intervention, in order to convince other nations of the critical importance of avoiding an export credit war.

# Part IV
# International Investment

# 8 Toward Greater Cooperation in International Investment Policies

More than ever before, investment has become an engine of future economic growth and a key factor influencing future trade flows. Increased domestic investment has become a common objective of all nations, including the United States. We need more investment to support more jobs, more exports, more productive capacity to fight inflation, and new technologies.

Investment across national borders can be a major contributor to achieving these objectives. The United States has, therefore, traditionally supported and currently maintains an open policy toward both outward and inward private investment.

In promoting these objectives, however, governments at both federal and subfederal levels frequently adopt measures which can distort the allocation of investment among nations, reduce the potential gains from international specialization, and prompt countermeasures by other governments. Key problems involve the use of financial, trade, tax, and other incentives to attract foreign investment which might otherwise locate elsewhere, and the imposition of performance requirements which seek to tilt the economic benefits stemming from particular investments to one country at the expense of others.

However, there is at present virtually no international regulation of government actions in the investment field—no guidelines for what is acceptable, no recognized recourse against harmful actions by others. The problems resulting from government interference in this area are proliferating and will become even more troublesome in the decade ahead. Improved international cooperation is essential.

I would like to discuss some of the most important problems we face concerning international investment, the progress we have achieved so far in enhancing cooperation, and some ideas about further steps in this key area.

## Investment Issues

Government intervention regarding international investment tends to follow a carrot-and-stick approach: luring foreign investment into the domes-

Originally presented on February 28, 1980, before the American Law Institute/American Bar Association in New York, New York.

tic economy through artificial investment incentives, tied to the imposition of performance requirements to assure that the investment meets specific economic or social objectives of the host nation. The result is often an implicit alliance between multinational corporations and host countries. This result can run counter to the national interest of the corporation's home country, or to other countries whose economies are adversely affected, or to the interest of private competitors of the firm in question. Intervention by one nation begets intervention by others, and risks conflict between governments as they vie with each other for jobs, production, and exports.

International competition for investment projects is becoming an expensive habit, paid for from the pockets of domestic consumers and the potential profits of "losing" firms. The use of investment incentives is spreading and has already generated some government-to-government clashes.

Emulation is especially visible in the auto sector. The offer of investment incentives has become a key factor in winning new auto plants, often in competition with others:

> In 1978, Canada paid the Ford Motor Company $68 million to build a plant in Ontario instead of Ohio.
>
> Last year, France reportedly offered Ford in the neighborhood of $400 million to locate an automotive assembly plant in Alsace-Lorraine, as it bid against other countries for a project that eventually was abandoned.
>
> Nigeria has offered $70 million in equity and loans to British Leyland.
>
> Within the United States, tax and other incentives amounting to $80 million were extended to Volkswagen for its Rabbit assembly plant in Pennsylvania.

Performance requirements have also been developed to a high degree of sophistication in many countries. Advanced developing countries, such as Brazil and Mexico, require foreign companies to produce locally up to 100 percent of the value-added as a condition of participation in their automobile industries—performance requirements which are equivalent to zero import quotas on parts and other imports and which are relaxed only if the companies expand their exports. The Mexican Automotive Decree also levies export expansion requirements.

In another recent case, the Spanish Government combined import benefits and export performance requirements as part of a broader package to stimulate auto investment in Spain destined primarily for export. The incentives included a reduction in value-added requirements, duty free imports of parts, tax holidays, and the right of eminent domain in establishing a plant site. Ford's Fiesta plant in Spain now ships two-thirds of its production into export and has become that nation's largest foreign exchange earner.

Pressures are growing in the United States to adopt similar performance requirements to get foreign auto companies to locate here. The United Auto Workers and some U.S. auto companies sought additions to the Energy Policy and Conservation Act of 1975 which would have imposed local content requirements on such plants and their production in the United States to ensure the use of U.S. parts and labor. In response to the dramatic increase in U.S. imports of Japanese automobiles, UAW President Douglas Fraser has recently proposed that Japanese auto firms be required by legislation to build plants in the United States and has revived the union's efforts to obtain local content requirements. An official of the Ford Motor Company has advocated a combination of import restrictions and local content requirements. The risk of further emulation is real.

Investment incentives and performance requirements such as these can and do distort basic investment decisions and subsequent trade flows. They can have the effect of shifting the location and benefits of investment across national borders, thereby exporting the problems of the country using them to others. They offer a form of preferential access to domestic markets for firms which will produce their inputs within a nation's borders rather than import them from other countries. The link to trade flows is a key indicator of the impact of investment measures on overall economic efficiency. By the time trade flows, however, irreversible decisions have been made and the damage is extremely difficult to undo.

## Need for Cooperation

A major objective of U.S. policy during the past three years has therefore been to achieve increased multilateral discipline on incentives and other interventions by governments, both to maintain an open investment environment and to avoid emulative countermeasures. The 1976 OECD Declaration on International Investment and Multinational Enterprises deals with aspects of the problem. Although limited in its scope and impact, it represents a significant first step in creating multilateral agreement and increasing international cooperation on investment issues. Bilateral investment treaties and treaties of friendship, commerce, and navigation deal with some aspects of the investment relationship. None of these, however, constitutes more than a start at achieving international cooperation in this area.

We now have an international code governing the use of subsidies and countervailing duties—one of the most important accomplishments of the recent round of Multilateral Trade Negotiations. We do not have a code for investment incentives or performance requirements. We should. Even more basic, but more long-term in nature, we should have a "GATT for investment" similar to the general agreement on tariffs and trade (GATT) we now have for trade: a common body of rights and regulations which defines acceptable actions and provides recourse for those whose rights are harmed. Such an arrangement would not necessarily embody a single international institution, like the GATT for trade—but it should embody rules of the game and institutional arrangements which would serve as a functional equivalent.

Most governments have not yet recognized the importance of increased cooperation in this area. In part, this is because direct investment has become a major vehicle for international economic exchange only in the last twenty years or so, and its impact upon the international economy has thus not been visible for as long a time as the impact of trade flows and monetary developments. In addition, the lack of readily available data in this area means that nations do not realize the extent of government intervention in investment, the degree of emulation which is already occurring, and the potential impact of these actions on future trade flows and overall economic relations. As in the trade field, before the development of the GATT, nobody knew the extent of trade barriers that had been erected in the 1930s—until the roof fell in.

Unaddressed, the underlying problems resulting from governments' use of incentives and performance requirements will likely get worse. The volume of international investments is growing rapidly. The general trend toward growing government intervention and increasing interdependence builds pressures to export one's problems.

If experience with the interplay of national economic policies has taught us anything, it should be that we need to identify and devise means to address such problems at an early stage—before a crisis is required to bring forth appropriate international action. Failure to take international action in the 1930s led to trade wars and competitive exchange rate devaluations, actions which deepened and prolonged the Great Depression. Only after the Depression were trade and monetary rules created that were designed to prevent the recurrence of this kind of cut-throat competition—rules that have succeeded remarkably well. In the investment area, we should begin work now to ensure that individual nations' actions not precipitate similar developments.

### Developments to Date

Some progress has been made toward greater cooperation in these areas over the past few years.

First, as a result of their review of the 1976 Investment Declaration, the member countries of the OECD have embarked on a Medium Term Work Program on investment incentives and disincentives. The first stage of this program will consist of an analysis of the effects of such measures on the international investment process. The second will deal with their impact on international economic relations. We hope that this effort will result in agreement on more effective ways to deal with problems in this area among the OECD countries, which are both homes and hosts to most of the world's international investment.

Second, an Investment Task Force which I chair has been created under the auspices of the Development Committee, an intergovernmental group under the combined auspices of the International Monetary Fund and the World Bank. This task force of representatives from both industrialized and developing nations is searching for specific steps which might be taken to improve the contribution of direct investment to the development process, including the possibility of new international arrangements to limit the use of incentives and performance requirements.

Third, the United States has been engaged in bilateral talks with Canada over the use of investment incentives in the automobile industry. These discussions stem originally from U.S. government protests over the Canadian grant to Ford in August 1978 but relate more broadly to the traditionally close cooperation between our two countries in the automotive sector. We hope that these talks will ultimately result in agreement between the United States and our close neighbor to limit such incentives.

Fourth, the British minister of industry, Mr. Keith Joseph, has publicly indicated the British government's interest in achieving an agreement regulating the use of incentives to bid for internationally mobile investments.

Fifth, Brazil's recent decisions to eliminate immediately its major export subsidies and to participate in the new subsidy code exemplifies an improved willingness on the part of a key developing country to consider the international impact of domestic measures and to gradually eliminate artificial practices which could harm foreign industries as Brazilian industries become internationally competitive.

## A "GATT for Investment"

It is impossible to predict the form that international cooperation in the investment area might ultimately take. I use the term "GATT for investment" to convey the concept of an overall body of rules and institutional arrangements to govern international investment. The term does not necessarily mean a new institution solely for investment purposes. It could well be a series of arrangements grafted onto existing international bodies.

Such a GATT for investment need not be elaborate or comprehensive in its initial stages. It could build upon the progress already underway and evolve gradually into a comprehensive set of international regulations governing investment actions. It would not happen overnight, but would reflect a common recognition of the need for cooperation and embody a series of individual steps, taken both multilaterally and bilaterally, toward this common objective.

Initial steps toward a GATT for investment could include agreement in the following areas:

1. transparency of current investment measures
2. notification of any future measures which might be adopted
3. a standstill on current measures or levels of measures
4. over time, a rollback of existing investment measures

Similar commitments provided the original basis for the development of the GATT for trade—an agreement which has evolved into a widely accepted set of international rights and obligations, a formal organization for discussion of common problems, and specific dispute resolution procedures. The basic framework of the GATT has been revised and expanded to meet the needs of today's rapidly changing world economy through the recent Multilateral Trade Negotiations. Members now include more than eighty nations which account for over three-fourths of world trade.

## Other Models

Besides the GATT for trade, there are a number of other models to consider as building blocks. Two of the most important are the new code on subsidies and countervailing measures, and the European Community's internal experience in regulating investment incentives.

The subsidies code provides an immediate basis for getting at some investment incentives and performance requirements which can cause injury to other nations. It incorporates the triple requirements of transparency, notification, and consultation.

Domestic subsidies are explicitly recognized as countervailable subsidies under the new code, provided injury is shown. Nations agree to seek to avoid causing serious prejudice to other nations in using subsidies to eliminate industrial, economic, and social disadvantages in specific regions, to facilitate the restructuring of certain sectors, to sustain employment and encourage retraining and change in employment, or to encourage research and development programs. They also agree to consider possible adverse effects of such measures on trade and existing conditions of world trade, production, and supply in the product concerned. Examples of general kinds of subsidies understood to be covered by the code include government financing of commercial enterprises, including grants, loans, or guarantees; government or government-financed provision of utility, supply distribution, and other operational or support services or facilities; government financing of research and development programs; fiscal incentives; and government subscription to or provision of equity capital.

Nations also have the right to retaliate against domestic subsidies which impair GATT tariff bindings for which reciprocal concessions have been negotiated. Such subsidies become an alternative to tariff protection to restrict access to domestic markets.

Within the broad category of subsidies is a specific set of practices classified as "export subsidies." Signatories commit themselves not to grant export subsidies on products other than certain primary products. The "export subsidy" concept singles out those subsidy practices which differentiate between sales destined for domestic markets and sales destined for export markets. Prohibited export subsidies specifically include the provision by governments of direct subsidies to a firm or industry contingent upon export performance.

These rules, however, are effective only after trade begins to flow and injury can be shown. Trade sanctions, such as countervailing duties, have traditionally been taken after production is underway and trade is established, long after millions of dollars are invested in a facility and jobs are transferred from one location to another. When that kind of damage has already been done, the usefulness of trade sanctions as a remedy for the injury is quite limited.

A major objective in the investment area would be to move the coverage of international discipline back from the point at which trade flows to the actual investment decision, and to apply it to potential distortions on the import as well as the export side.

The second key "model" is the European Community's (EC) system of rules which places a limit on the investment aids granted by the member countries to assure that there will be no distortion of competition in the production of goods within the Community as a whole. The rules have evolved gradually on a selective basis but now provide for a general surveillance role for the EC Commission. The Commission's authority extends in particular to (1) regional aids designed to offset special handicaps (that is, low standard of living, serious unemployment) or to facilitate the development of certain economic areas; and (2) sectoral aids designed to facilitate the development or restructuring of certain industries or to promote an important project of common EC interest.

The Commission's powers involve regular review, a requirement for prenotification of new projects or changes in current projects, a right to initiate an examination or require information to be supplied by member countries to make sure that the agreed limits on investment incentives have not been exceeded, and the power to rule that proposed aids are incompatible with the Treaty of Rome. Member countries that do not comply with Commission decisions may be taken to the EC Court of Justice. The EC experience has demonstrated the importance of transparency—or measurability—in member country investment aids and the need to distinguish between aids which distort competition in an adverse manner and those which are beneficial.

Would it be possible to generalize the EC rule, at least to the OECD nations? Could the OECD be an institutional reference point similar to the EC Commission within the Community? Is this a path we might want to pursue?

It is no accident that investment rules have developed most fully where free trade exists, as within the European Community. Once nations have ruled out the use of trade barriers among themselves, governments are increasingly tempted to influence trade flows via investment policies. Investment rules are necessary, therefore, to restrict the use of investment distortions and thereby complement and maintain the benefits of the open trade arrangement.

**Defining Acceptable Measures**

In designing a GATT for investment we will also have to devise a basis for defining acceptable and unacceptable investment measures. In the incentive area, we might ask:

> When is an incentive legitimate as a means to offset the disadvantage of investing in a particular locale, and when does it exceed that bound?
>
> When does an incentive actually induce a firm to shift production from one nation to another, as opposed to influencing where among several sites within a nation it might locate?

We do not have clear answers to these questions. However, two principles can be tentatively put forth: an undesirable investment incentive would be one which would both

1. Cause industrial investment to be located in the territory of the nation granting the incentive, while in the absence of the incentive the investment would go to some other nation's territory, and
2. Distort the efficient allocation of resources as between any pair of nations.

It should be noted that, under these principles, measures which are sometimes referred to as "incentives," but in fact amount to the removal of government-imposed disincentives to investment, would not be condemned. Such exempt measures, for example, would include broad-based tax reductions and the liberalization of government regulations which affect business. These measures would constitute a move by government toward a "neutral" role in investment decisions. If one government moves toward "neutrality," it should be above criticism by other governments. By contrast, direct or indirect subsidies to a firm which are not compensatory in nature—including operating subsidies, subsidized loans, free provision, or payment of front end cash or noncash grants to the firm—would be covered.

Two categories of incentives may require special treatment. One encompasses incentives designed to draw investment into disadvantaged or depressed regions of a nation. The other covers incentives to research and development. Arguments based on sound economic reasoning suggest that a limited case might be made for direct subsidies in each of these areas. Even here, however, limits on the use of such incentives are necessary, as EC experience has shown. Maximum subsidies in the European Community for aid to depressed regions generally have been limited to 20 percent of the total project.

Dealing with performance requirements is at least as difficult as dealing with investment incentives. In general terms, it can be argued on economic grounds that any performance requirement is undesirable unless it acts to offset some imperfection in the working of the market.

The problem is to determine what, if any, imperfections exist in a given situation and to determine if performance requirements act solely to correct the deficiency. Such a determination is particularly thorny in the case of some developing countries. Performance requirements are often justified as necessary to offset the alleged market power of multinational enterprises and thereby assure that they meet the goals of host governments. But abuses by multinational firms in developing nations are exaggerated, and we believe that the case for performance requirements is vastly overstated.

## Coverage of States, Localities

A lesson which a number of nations are increasingly recognizing is that all levels of government need to be involved in this cooperative effort, including the U.S. states, the Canadian provinces, and the German *Länder*. Indeed, many of our states are already uneasy over the competition among themselves for new investments—a process quite similar to the international situation I have been describing. During one discussion of this topic, a state development official commented that "we wasted $5 billion last year in subsidizing private firms."

The United States cannot afford, at either the federal or state levels of government, to ignore the effects of state actions on American economic relations with other countries. In the past, a foreign firm usually made a strategic decision to invest in the United States, then it searched for a suitable location, often shopping between anxious states for the best bid. While this two-stage process was expensive for the bidding state, it did not create international difficulties. But with the increasing internationalization of production, foreign countries have frequently become attractive alternatives for servicing the American market. The states, therefore, now often find themselves competing with foreign governments—as well as with each other—in bidding for an individual plant.

Foreign governments have also competed with U.S. subfederal governments for investments by U.S. firms. In mid-1978, the DeLorean Motor Company was close to final agreement with the government of Puerto Rico to establish an automobile plant in return for an incentive package consisting of a loan, loan guarantees, and a training grant. In August 1978, however, DeLorean announced its intention to set up a plant in Northern Ireland in return for an incentive package which included grants, loans, and other inducements worth more than $100 million.

The Canadian grant to the Ford Motor Company offers another example of this kind of competition. The Canadian government contended that it was forced to compete with an incentive that Ford was being offered by the State of Ohio. United States complaints over that action have led to discussion on cooperative means of curbing the use of incentives by governments on both sides of the border. A particularly difficult issue, of concern to both Canada and the United States, is how any agreement might apply to the state and provincial governments.

Although it involves state restrictions on—rather than incentives to—foreign investment, a court case in Oklahoma raises important questions about the role of the states in the international investment process. The attorney general of Oklahoma has ruled that land in the state owned by foreign corporations legally belongs to the state because a provision in the Oklahoma constitution bars such ownership. Pursuant to the ruling, he has ordered a Canadian firm that is one of the largest commercial property owners in the state to divest itself of its holdings or face escheat proceedings.

In response, suits have been filed by the Canadian firm and the U.S. Chamber of Commerce, on behalf of the state's Chamber of Commerce and another local business group. The latter suit is intended to overturn the ruling on the grounds that it violates several provisions of the U.S. Constitution, including the interstate commerce clause. The implications of the outcome could be quite far-reaching.

In other areas where progress has been achieved in curbing or studying federal practices, state and local practices are either explicitly or implicity included. The OECD medium-term study of investment incentives and disincentives will cover the practices of all levels of government: local, state, and national. The United States intends to use the new subsidy code's provisions in its efforts to limit the subsidy practices of foreign governments at both federal and subfederal levels. Other signatories can be expected to do the same with regard to American subsidy practices.

Under these and other agreements, subfederal units will be affected to varying degrees. Under some agreements, the states do not have formal obligations but their economic policies may be subject to foreign retaliation. Under other agreements, a direct challenge to state policies may be mounted in the U.S. courts. In any event, both the state and federal governments will be involved in the notification, consultation, and dispute settlement phases of these problems.

## Conclusion

The United States has a basic national interest in seeking improved international cooperation in the investment field.

As a home country for U.S. industries, we do not want to see our industries lured abroad by foreign incentives that deprive the U.S. economy of jobs, income, and export earnings. Performance requirements imposed on U.S. firms investing abroad can also decrease exports from the United States and increase sales back to our market.

As a host country to foreign investment, we are concerned about the dual problems of competition for investment among our own states and assuring that foreign investment which would benefit U.S. jobs and industrial production is not lured elsewhere.

Investment is an essential determinant of economic growth and a key element in trade flows. Cooperation in this area is as important as in trade monetary affairs. We are encouraged that progress is being made. We will continue to work for more progress in the future.

# 9 Foreign Investment in the United States

The Reciprocity in Foreign Investment Act (H.R. 7791) has the potential to affect foreign direct investment in the United States significantly. I will therefore briefly review current U.S. policy; comment on some criticisms thereof; and, finally, indicate why the administration opposes H.R. 7791.

## U.S. Policy

It is the fundamental policy of the U.S. government to welcome foreign investment to this country and extend national treatment to foreign-owned firms based in the United States. However, we do not actively promote—nor of course do we discourage—inward or outward international investment. We believe that foreign investment, like all investment, makes a maximum contribution to society when it responds to market forces. We therefore believe that the government should normally avoid measures which give special incentives or disincentives to investment flows or to the activities of individual companies regarding international investment.

This policy was officially articulated by the administration in a statement issued in July 1977 after a careful review of both inward and outward investment policy by the Economic Policy Group, the administration's top policy-making body for all economic issues. The statement reaffirmed the long-standing U.S. commitment to an open international economic system, which has been applied to incoming direct investment throughout our two centuries of national history.

## Benefits of U.S. Policy

This policy has served our nation well. Increased investment is an objective of all nations, including the United States. It means more jobs, more productive capacity, and more technology. It means more exports and more capital inflows to strengthen the balance of payments and the dollar. It means more competition to help combat inflation.

---

Originally presented on September 9, 1980, before the Subcommittee on Consumer Protection and Finance of the Committee on Interstate and Foreign Commerce of the U.S. House of Representatives.

The ability of the United States to attract foreign investment to help achieve such goals has been substantial. There has been a dramatic increase in foreign investment in the United States during the 1970s. As measured on a balance-of-payments basis, the level rose from just under $12 billion at the end of 1967 to over $52 billion at the end of 1979. Much of this 300 percent increase is due to the substantial inflows that occurred in 1973-1974 ($10.3 billion) and in 1978-1979 ($17.6 billion).

Another measure of the extent of foreign investment here is the total assets of foreign investors. Recently, the U.S. Department of Commerce published the results of a survey of the nonbank U.S. affiliates of foreign companies in the United States. They reported that the total assets of such enterprises were $131 billion at the end of 1977—as compared to about $84 billion in 1974. Those companies employed more than a million people in 1977, with total compensation of nearly $17.5 billion. They also spent about $900 million for research and development. As indicated by the growth in the balance-of-payments measurement, all these figures are undoubtedly much higher now. In sum, the United States has already become a very attractive site for internationally mobile investment—to the envy of the rest of the world.

**Fear of Foreign Control**

Since the early 1970s, concerns have occasionally been expressed that there is too much foreign investment in the United States and that foreign countries through their investments here may take control of the U.S. economy—or at least important sectors of it. Those fears are plainly absurd. Despite the substantial *amounts* of foreign investment in the United States, foreign interests control an extremely small *share* of the U.S. capital stock.

The Commerce Department has estimated that, in 1977, U.S. affiliates of foreign corporations accounted for only 2 percent of the employment of all U.S. businesses except banks. They accounted for less than one-half of one percent of privately owned U.S. land. They accounted for 2.6 percent of the total value-added for the U.S. economy as a whole.

These percentages have clearly risen a bit in the last two years, but they are still tiny. The numbers are tinier yet for the OPEC countries, which are sometimes singled out for particular concern; they own something like .01 of 1 percent of the capital stock of U.S. companies.

It is also curious to observe U.S. fears regarding foreign influence over our national economic interest in light of the vastly higher proportion of businesses in other countries owned by foreign—predominantly U.S.—firms. In Canada, for example, over 55 percent of manufacturing industry is owned by foreigners, as is 31 percent of its nonfinancial industry. United States firms alone control 43 percent of Canadian manufacturing. The number is somewhat lower in Europe and in big developing countries such as Mexico or Brazil, but they are far higher than the tiny ratios of foreign ownership here in the United States.

Despite the relatively huge ownership interests of U.S. firms in various foreign countries, these countries—with the occasional exception of Canada—do not exhibit the kinds of fears which are now occasionally voiced in the United States. There *was* concern in Europe a decade ago over "Le Defi Americain"; that concern has now virtually disappeared. Nearly all countries have learned that ownership does not imply control, nor does control require ownership. In most foreign countries, concern over foreign ownership has diminished to a point where it is no longer a major issue.

## Global Trends

For that same reason, however, there are some important and disturbing global trends with respect to national policies toward foreign investment. Governments at both the federal and subfederal levels are seeking to both attract and control the impact of such investment (rather than worry about who owns it). In so doing they are adopting measures which can distort the allocation of investment among nations, reduce the gains from international specialization, reallocate the benefits of investment from one country to another, and prompt countermeasures by other governments.

Major problems arise from two related directions. One is the use by governments of financial, trade, tax, and other incentives to attract foreign investment, which might otherwise locate elsewhere, and thus rearrange the location of production. The second is their imposition of performance requirements which seek to tilt the economic benefits stemming from particular investments to one country at the expense of others.

A critical question for U.S. policy, now and in the future, is whether to emulate this trend ourselves or to continue to oppose it, that is, should we fight them or join them? It seems clear to this administration that we should fight them and not reverse our policy by erecting barriers to the free flow of investment and other activities.

The economic and political price of such a reversal would be high. As I have already noted, we have an open door for foreign investment in this country because such investment provides new productive capacity, new technologies, and more exports to create jobs, strengthen the dollar, help improve our balance of payments, and fight inflation. These needs are particularly apparent now. A policy reversal would, in all likelihood, discourage foreign investments in the United States and be particularly damaging to the U.S. economic well-being.

In addition, a reversal in U.S. policy would redound to the disadvantage of U.S. investment abroad. These investments now total over $190 billion. Income from them strengthened our current account by $37.8 billion last year, fully offsetting our deficit on merchandise trade and thus sustaining the dollar. It would be sheer folly to invite negative foreign actions toward this huge stock of U.S.-owned investment.

At the international level, a reversal of U.S. policy would almost certainly kill our efforts to develop new agreements governing the use of incentives and performance requirements which, as noted already, are important problems with potentially adverse effects on the U.S. economy. The United States is the leader in pressing for agreement in these areas; if we changed course, the effort would collapse. We fully recognize that progress in this fight against government measures which distort international investment will take time, but we believe that progress is being made.

Governments are becoming more aware of the potential dangers of a proliferation of these measures, and are beginning to recognize the importance of increased cooperation in this area. As testimony to this increased awareness and cooperation, I would like to give the Subcommittee a brief report on the activities of a Task Force on Private Foreign Investment of the Development Committee of the IMF and World Bank which I have had the pleasure of chairing. The Committee established the Task Force in late 1978 to examine home and host government policies that affect the direct investment process and development. The Task Force, composed of developed and developing country representatives, will be presenting its final report to the next meeting of the Development Committee here in Washington—in conjunction with the annual meetings of the IMF and World Bank—in late September. Despite the diverse interests and policies of the countries represented, the Task Force *inter alia:*

> recognized that performance requirements, although they are designed to enable host countries to ensure that they obtain adequate benefits from incoming investments, may in some cases work to their disadvantage and may also, under certain circumstances, discourage investment or produce distortions in the economy of the host country;
>
> noted that, in view of the widespread use of incentives by host countries, countries offering them may not do much to improve their competitive position but rather may simply increase the profits of the firms and the taxes paid to the investors' home country treasuries;
>
> agreed that the use of performance requirements and incentives by one country may have adverse effects on others, for instance, by diverting

investment from other countries to their own, thus provoking retaliation and/or emulation by the "losing" countries;

noted in this connection that performance requirements could become tantamount to a restrictive trade practice and more generally cause distortions in trade flows;

endorsed the objectives of seeking an international understanding which would limit the adverse effects of incentives and of considering what further actions might need to be taken concerning performance requirements and decided in some detail what an arrangement to limit incentives could look like; and

recommended that the World Bank Group study and analyze existing foreign investment incentives and performance requirements and, depending on the outcome of the study, consider making an attempt to develop a concept and terms upon which an understanding to limit the adverse effects of such measures might evolve.

This is a modest, but significant, step toward dealing with today's real problems concerning international investment. All countries represented recognized the need to focus on the issue and are committed to do so. Having led this effort so far, the United States should not jeopardize it by acting unilaterally to deter incoming foreign investment.

## H.R. 7791

With all this as preamble, let me now focus on H.R. 7791. The proposal takes a more moderate approach to monitoring and controlling foreign direct investment in the United States than other proposals that have been put forward. Nonetheless, it raises many problems:

1. It would be taken around the world as a signal that the United States had shifted its historic position and become less open to incoming foreign investment. It would therefore clearly discourage such investment, denying us the kind of benefits outlined earlier at a time when these benefits—jobs, capital, technology, exports—are sorely needed.

2. It would produce an impossible administrative task: investors from several countries with diverse investment policies wishing to invest in the same U.S. industry or company would be subject to completely different rules, based on each foreign government's policies with respect to their incoming foreign investment.

3. Such action would clearly undermine the progress we have made thus far in attacking the major problems of incentives and performance

requirements and would almost certainly jeopardize any future attempts to arrive at a multilateral agreement in this area.

4. Other countries would react negatively to such legislation, making conditions worse for U.S. investment abroad and perhaps, even jeopardizing the massive flow of direct investment income which is a great source of strength for the dollar and our balance of payments.

For these reasons, the administration opposes H.R. 7791.

# Part V
# The Developing Countries in the World Economy

# 10 North-South Relations: A Candid Appraisal

Economic and political relations between the industrialized North and the developing South have improved dramatically since the early 1970s. Six years ago, both the tone and substance of North-South relations were characterized by confrontation and hostility. A number of developing nations sought to force a radical restructuring of the world economic system. They proposed to jettison existing international economic institutions and impose a series of unilateral rights of the developing nations as the sole criterion for a "New International Economic Order" (NIEO).

Most industrialized nations, particularly the United States, found both the manner and the substance of these demands offensive and economically unacceptable. Some sincerely believed that the new demands of the developing countries were not in the interest of the developing countries themselves. Some resisted change simply because they found the status quo to be quite comfortable. Some believed that reform was possible, and perhaps necessary, but rightly believed that it could not come about through open confrontation and shrill rhetoric.

Fortunately, moderate voices and a willingness to consider the realistic needs of North and South alike emerged over time in both the North and South. After considerable effort and negotiations in a variety of international fora there has occurred a great deal of international economic reform—to the substantial benefit of both North and South. To be sure, problems remain in North-South relations. But the record of the recent past demonstrates clearly that North and South can work together successfully to resolve common problems and assure that an evolving international economic system provides mutual benefits for all nations.

I want to analyze in some detail this rather dramatic change in international affairs and then suggest that the most urgent task for North-South relations now is to build on that record of progress and to avoid any relapse to the sterile stand-off of just a few years ago.

## The Early 1970s: Confrontation

The confrontation of the early 1970s derived from strong differences in perceptions of the benefits flowing from the international economic system, as well as sharply divergent international economic goals. Shrill demands

Originally presented on January 29, 1980, before the Center for Inter-American Relations in New York City.

for a "New International Economic Order" to transfer resources unilaterally to the developing nations were made by many developing countries. These nations, largely using the highly politicized fora provided by the United Nations, harangued the North for economic imperialism and exploitation. They pushed through controversial resolutions—such as the NEIO and the Charter for Economic Rights and Duties of States—which were unacceptable to the United States and other industrialized countries.

Developing country tactics were matched by rigid resistance on the part of the United States and some other industrialized nations. They adopted the view that few, if any, changes in the international economic system were needed. Rhetoric was high on both sides. There was little interest in negotiating meaningfully to find common ground.

Feeling both defensive and aggravated, the United States in particular was unwilling to even talk about a number of issues which seemed of critical importance to developing countries. This list included problems involving individual commodities, the establishment of a Common Fund, monetary matters, and problems surrounding international investment and multinational corporations. The United States put a flat ceiling on the lending program of the World Bank. United States concessional aid flows fell to their lowest point since World War II.

The developing nations therefore reasoned, understandably to some extent, that cooperation with the industrialized countries—particularly with the leading industrialized country, the United States—was unlikely to produce achievement of some of their most fundamental goals. The negotiating option simply would not work, as they saw it. Rhetoric and intransigence precluded it as a viable option. Hence, confrontation was the only available vehicle to pursue their national goals.

The dramatic emergence of OPEC as a world power was also a heady experience for the developing nations. Many of them viewed OPEC's success as a model to emulate in their relations with the North, as well as a source of direct support for their own economic and political goals. A number of developing countries sought to form cartels for such commodities as bauxite, coffee, and copper. The developed nations heard the South's rhetoric and feared concerted third world action. This fear, coupled with the South's sense of triumph, heightened the mood of confrontation and made each side stand firmer in its respective position.

### The Late 1970s: Cooperation

Fortunately, overall North-South relations have changed considerably since those traumatic days. There has been significant improvement in both substance and tone as positions were moderated on both sides—an improvement from which all countries can derive great satisfaction.

Former Secretary of State Kissinger's speech in September 1975 before the Seventh Special Session of the UN General Assembly was the first sign that U.S. policy toward the developing nations was changing. In that speech, the United States called for an end to confrontation between developed and developing countries and for a new mode of international cooperation to ensure basic economic security for all nations. To this end, it proposed a number of new initiatives. Among them were proposals to stablize countries' export earnings, a point of particular importance to less developed countries (LDCs); to assist LDCs in gaining access to long-term capital markets; to facilitate exchange of technological information; and to develop additional energy resources.

This new U.S. approach began to defuse the confrontational rhetoric and set the tone for serious negotiations on substantive issues. The United States joined the international tin and coffee agreements in 1976. The United States was instrumental in securing substantial liberalization of the Compensatory Financing Facility (CFF) of the International Monetary Fund (IMF), which met one of the major needs of the developing countries—a balance-of-payments financing mechanism to help see them through periods of temporary shortfalls in export earnings. The result was immediate: drawings by developing countries alone during the world economic downturn in 1976-1977 increased to $1.9 billion, more than the $1.2 billion drawn by the IMF membership as a whole during the entire preceding thirteen years of the facility.

The agreement of industrialized, developing, and oil-producing nations to discuss a wide range of economic issues through the Conference on International Economic Cooperation (CIEC) beginning in 1975 revealed this new emphasis on cooperation in resolving common problems. In hindsight, we can see that the CIEC tried to focus on too many issues in disparate fields and to do so through political negotiations removed from the functionally specific international fora where successful results are much more likely. CEIC was, however, an important learning experience for North and South alike.

## The Objectives of U.S. Policy

Coming into office during the final phase of the CIEC experience, the Carter administration was determined to achieve widespread progress in North-South relations. It concluded, however, that comprehensive global negotiations would not promote this objective. Substantive progress could only come from diligent efforts in each of the key functional areas, based on an appreciation of the potential joint gains for both North and South from such efforts.

The new U.S. policy toward the developing countries was based upon three considerations:

1. The growing importance of the developing countries to U.S. security and foreign policy interests;
2. the importance of the developing countries to U.S. economic interests; and
3. the potential for mutual gains through a cooperative North-South approach in specific policy areas.

The developing countries have assumed an increasingly important role in world affairs. A number of global problems of great importance to the United States can be resolved only with the cooperation of the developing countries. The Soviet invasion of Afghanistan and the taking of U.S. hostages in Iran are clear cases in point, where LDC support—whether through votes on key resolutions in the United Nations, or in cooperation with direct U.S. responses, or in other ways—is vital to fundamental U.S. security and political interests. It is a simple truism to recognize that the prospects for LDC support on such issues of primary importance to the United States will be enhanced by U.S. cooperation on issues of keen interest to them.

In a similar manner, U.S. economic interests require effective relations with the developing countries. The United States sell more than 20 percent of its exports to nonoil developing countries, equivalent to $34 billion in 1978. Twenty-five percent of U.S. manufactured exports went to nonoil, developing countries in 1978, more than to the entire European Community. More than half a million U.S. manufacturing jobs produce for export to nonoil LDCs. The United States is highly dependent upon the developing countries for supplies of crucial raw materials and a number of tropical agricultural products.

This increasing economic interdependence offers considerable potential for joint gains in a number of areas. Energy price and availability, for example, have been a crucial problem for all oil-importing countries—industrialized and developing. Trade offers potential for growing markets and increased specialization for North and South alike with a resulting increase in global efficiency, stimulus to economic growth and employment, and lower consumer costs. Greater commodity price stability benefits both producers and consumers. Development assistance can provide the needed stimulus for economic growth which will eventually enable the LDCs to attract private capital and begin importing foreign manufactured goods, as well as manifesting our humanitarian desires to better the lives of people everywhere.

**The Recent Record**

The United States, particularly since 1977, has therefore adopted a positive and comprehensive approach to North-South economic relations. This change in U.S. attitudes has made possible common action by the industrialized nations as a group. This in turn has revived the prospects for the cooperative approach to North-South relations and made possible the improvement of recent years.

Progress has been made on a number of fronts. In the last two years, new multilateral initiatives undertaken by the industrialized countries acting together will make almost $100 billion in additional funds available to the developing countries. Some of these funds are in the form of concessional assistance. Some represent intermediation in the private capital markets. Some offer short-term balance-of-payments support, as part of efforts to improve the functioning of the international monetary system for the benefit of all countries. All provide real economic assistance to those nations. In addition, we have negotiated a series of nonquantifiable breakthroughs in such areas as trade and commodity policy. These achievements are all the more impressive in light of the economic difficulties which have beset both the United States and most other national economies during this period. Let me enumerate.

*Multilateral Development Banks (MDBs)*

The United States has supported a capital increase for the World Bank of $40 billion. We took the lead in negotiating a replenishment of almost $10 billion for the Inter-American Development Bank. We participated in negotiating a new replenishment of over $2 billion for the Asian Development Fund and have agreed to U.S. membership in the African Development Bank (AFDB) and an increase in AFDB capital of $4.5 billion. For IDA, the soft loan window of the World Bank which is the most important concessional assistance institution in the world, we contributed 31 percent to the fifth replenishment of $7.6 billion in 1977 and have just pledged 27 percent to the sixth replenishment of $12 billion. To fulfill these pledges, the administration worked with Congress to obtain a record level of appropriations of $2.5 billion for fiscal 1979 for the MDBs, up from only $700 million voted for fiscal 1977 before this administration took office.

*Strengthened Monetary System*

The United States has supported a number of steps to strengthen the international monetary system and the International Monetary Fund (IMF), the central institution of the system. These steps are beneficial to all countries, developed and developing alike, for they ensure a strong financial structure to facilitate the expansion and balanced growth of the world economy.

As the world's central monetary institution, the IMF provides the basic framework for international monetary cooperation and makes financial resources available to all member countries in times of balance-of-payments need. The United States has supported a series of recent actions to strengthen the financial capabilities of the IMF to meet the demands on its resources in a period of rapid change and political strain.

The Supplementary Financial Facility, with resources amounting to about $10 billion, was established last year to supplement temporarily regular IMF assistance to countries with particularly severe payments problems; since its commencement last spring, arrangements for $1.8 billion have been agreed under the Facility—all for the benefit of developing countries.

An increase in members' quotas was implemented in early 1978, to further enhance the IMF's permanent resources, and an additional 50 percent increase in quotas is scheduled to take effect later this year—which, taken together, will increase LDC quotas by about $8.4 billion.

SDR allocations have been resumed, to help meet rising needs for world liquidity and promote the role of the SDR as the principal reserve asset in the monetary system. Over the period 1979-1981, nonoil, developing countries will receive allocations of about $3.6 billion.

The IMF's Compensatory Financing Facility has been further liberalized to provide temporary financing to countries experiencing a shortfall in export earnings caused by circumstances beyond their control. The Fund has lengthened the repayment period under its Extended Fund Facility to provide countries with more time in which to undertake major structural changes in their economies. And it is considering the possibility of lowering interest costs of the Supplementary Financing Facility.

### *Trade*

The United States reinvigorated the deadlocked Multilateral Trade Negotiations (MTN) and brought them to a successful conclusion. The resulting agreements provide a 25 percent cut in developed country tariffs applicable to LDC exports. United States tariff cuts on LDC products, excluding textiles and apparel, average about 35 percent.

New nontariff codes on subsidies, government procurement, standards, import licensing, and customs valuation will provide a much more open and stable environment for future trade growth. The agreements also provide a permanent legal basis for special and more favorable treatment of developing countries, accompanied by more liberal rules on trade measures taken for development purposes. Since opportunities for trade expansion are probably the single most important feature of the world economy for most developing nations, the MTN agreements mark an enormous step forward in North-South economic relations.

As probably the most important area of U.S. economic interaction with developing countries, trade provides the clearest example of mutual benefits for industrialized and developing countries alike. The nonoil LDCs are by far the fastest growing market for U.S. exports, where our sales have more than doubled from $16 billion in 1973 to over $34 in 1978.

At the same time, U.S. imports from developing countries grew from nearly $16 billion to $40 billion over this period. Despite the fact that the United States accounts for only about 40 percent of the combined GNP of the industrial countries, in 1978 the United States took more than 52 percent of developing country manufactured exports to all industrial countries. Nearly 22 percent of all our manufactured imports in 1978 came from developing countries; the corresponding figure for all other industrial countries was less than 5 percent. United States economic growth since the global recession of 1975 has been particularly beneficial to the nonoil LDCs, whose exports grew much faster to the U.S. market than to either Japan or the European Community.

### *Energy*

With strong support from the United States, the World Bank plans to support oil and gas projects totaling $7.7 billion over the next five years—which should produce an additional 2 million barrels of oil equivalent a day. Our own Overseas Private Investment Corporation (OPIC) has established political risk insurance for oil exploration, production, and development in developing countries, with significant results already. These multilateral and bilateral efforts will help reduce the dependence of developing countries on expensive oil imports and, at the same time, improve the world energy balance.

### *Commodities*

The United States supports the negotiation of stabilization agreements to dampen commodity price fluctuations, which can accelerate inflation for consuming countries and disrupt investment and production in producing countries. An international sugar agreement was finalized in September 1977. The framework of an agreement for the Common Fund was agreed on in March 1979. A rubber agreement was completed in October 1979. The United States, as a result of congressional action last month, will now contribute its share to the buffer stock of the tin agreement.

*Development Aid*

We and other donors have substantially increased concessional assistance to the poorer developing countries. Between 1970 and 1978, aid receipts by countries with per capita incomes below $400 have tripled. Measured in relation to the GNP of the recipient countries—which is probably the best overall indicator of the contribution of aid flows to a recipient's development—total official aid to the poor countries has sharply increased over the past few years. For the least developed countries, aid receipts increased from 2.6 percent of the recipients' combined GNP in 1969-1971 to 10.3 percent in 1978. For all countries with per capita GNP below $400, the growth was from 3.3 to 4.7 percent.

*Food*

The Carter administration joined in supporting the creation of a $1 billion International Fund for Agricultural Development (IFAD). United States farmers, acting on government incentives, placed 35 million tons of grain in reserve during 1977-1978; the value of this reserve was demonstrated last year when 14 million tons were released into the market in response to rising world demand. By ending the set-aside program in agriculture, we have helped provide more food for the world. We have proposed the creation of a special food aid reserve of four million tons of grain. We have pledged 4.5 million tons of food aid annually under the Food Aid Convention, nearly half of its 10-million-ton target. The United States has been in the forefront in urging the multilateral development banks to help develop effective food strategies; one-third of IBRD/IDA loans in 1980 will support LDC agricultural sectors, including rural development.

*Science and Technology*

The administration has proposed the establishment of an Institute for Scientific and Technological Cooperation (ISTC) to strengthen developing country capacity to conduct scientific and technological research on key development problems.

**The Responsibilities of the South**

All these developments provide concrete evidence of the willingness of the United States and the other industrialized countries to cooperate fully and in responding to the needs of the developing countries. The record clearly belies any view that the United States has been ungenerous in its help, or protectionist in its trade, or unresponsive to the needs of others.

As already indicated, we have taken these steps because we believe both in responding to the needs of others and in the prospects for mutual gains from properly conceived North-South relations. From our views concerning mutual gains, it follows naturally that we believe in mutual responsibility for the successful operation of the international economic system. It is in our interest, as well as that of the developing countries that they assume a greater role in the management of the global economy.

For example, a number of LDCs contributed substantially to the successful outcome of the MTN by liberalizing their own import regimes and agreeing to phase out their export subsidies. Several have become modest aid donors and now contribute to the same international lending agencies from which they borrowed only a few years ago. We expect that key developing countries will continue to make positive contributions in other international economic negotiations in the months and years ahead.

Latin America provides some of the best examples of the successful policy of mutual gains and shared responsibility. The majority of these countries—which are in the forefront of economic progress in the developing world—are no longer dependent on concessional aid. Some of these Latin American countries have begun to mount their own foreign assistance efforts to help the poorer nations in their midst.

To be sure, pockets of poverty and other severe development problems still exist in Latin America. But many of these countries are in the process of graduating from a position of dependency to full-fledged membership in the international economic system, making full use of private capital markets to finance their economic development and taking extensive advantage of world trading opportunities. The pace of such graduation has been slowed by the devastating impact of soaring oil prices, rampant inflation, and world economic slowdown. But its eventual culmination seems assured, and we welcome their rapid movement toward full participation in the world economy.

## Lessons for the Future

The primary lesson to be drawn from the progress achieved over the past five years is that the cooperative approach can work. With good will and hard work on both sides, mutual benefits can be derived from serious and flexible negotiation on specific issues of concern to all nations. The international economic order can be reformed in an evolutionary way to further the interest of all countries. Confrontation can be avoided.

But we must be alert to the risks of retrogression. We still occasionally hear harsh rhetoric concerning North-South relations and calls for unrealistic concession, reminiscent of the uglier period of six or seven years ago. Some cynics say that such rhetoric is harmless. Unfortunately, it is not. Such rhetoric is heard by North and South alike. It raises developing countries' expectations and thus their risk of disillusionment. The American people hear it, and conclude that developing countries are ungrateful for our assistance and insensitive to our own problems—thereby jeopardizing the prospects for sustaining our policy approach of the past few years.

Such rhetoric makes it difficult to work together toward common goals. Yet we know from recent history that a return to confrontation in North-South relations would not produce further progress. To the contrary, those relations would retrogress as a result.

Indeed, if the developing countries were to press for linkages between various negotiations, as some of their present rhetoric suggests, some would have us respond by withholding positive measures unless we are given something specific in return. We in the administration believe that this would be a bad approach, but we cannot ignore the pressures to pursue it which can result from irresponsible rhetoric from either North or South.

Unfortuantely, it is not only rhetoric, linkage, and incessant calls for the creation of new funds which would raise anew the specter of confrontation. Several developing countries seem again bent on seeking to control world markets for their commodity exports rather than working with consumers—within the framework of existing commodity agreements—to stabilize prices for the benefit of both. It is obviously imperative to avoid any such confrontation scenario, with industrialized and developing nations continuing to work pragmatically together to negotiate specific issues in their specific functional forums.

We have just begun, in the UN Committee of the Whole, to work out the substance and structure for a new round of economic negotiations. As we proceed in this endeavor, we should be careful to bear in mind the lessons of the past—that these negotiations have no chance of being fruitful unless they are undertaken in their proper functional fora with due regard for the national needs of both industrialized and developing countries. Politicizing the issues, and seeking simultaneous solutions to a multitude of problems, will only result in stalemate. As President Carter said in Caracas, in February 1978, "Real progress will come through specific, cooperative actions designed to meet specific needs—not through symbolic statements made by developing countries to recall past injustices. We need to share a responsibility for solving problems and not to divide the blame for ignoring problems."

Another important lesson we have learned since 1973 is that the oil-importing developing countries can hardly count on OPEC to champion their interests. Developing countries have in fact been ravaged by OPEC's actions. Many development plans have been severely constrained, or completely derailed, by the high cost of oil imports as well as by the indirect impact on developed countries caused by OPEC's actions.

In 1974 it took nearly 4 percent of LDC exports to pay for their oil imports. In 1980, we estimate that it will take 25 percent. Next year alone, the increase in the import bills of oil-importing LDCs due to higher energy prices will be $15 billion. Nonoil LDCs increasingly recognize that OPEC nations must contribute to resolving the common problems which their actions have helped to create.

## Conclusion

There has been considerable progress during the past few years in North-South relations. In the process of attaining this progress, we have sought to ensure that all the policies we have adopted will provide benefits for the United States as well as for the developing countries. Indeed, this is the only politically viable way in which such progress can be made.

The primary task before us now is to consolidate and make full use of those international economic instruments which have recently been put in place, most of which I have discussed. We can determine what further steps need to be taken only when we have implemented the new agreements and given them a chance to work.

At home, this requires rapid and faithful implementation—including by the Congress—of the various steps which have been worked out internationally. Abroad, it requires patience and perseverance in effectively utilizing the agreements of the late 1970s. By building on the progress made on specific issues in functionally specific fora over the past few years, we can hope to evolve a more stable and equitable world economy in the 1980s and beyond.

# 11 The Role of the Multilateral Development Banks

This is a presentation of the Carter administration's proposals for U.S. participation in the replenishment of resources of the International Development Association (IDA), for membership of the United States in the African Development Bank (AFDB) and subscriptions to that institution, and for changes in the budgetary and appropriations treatment of U.S. subscriptions to the callable capital of the World Bank (IBRD) and Asian Development Bank (ADB).

## The 1979 Legislation

I want to express the administration's appreciation for the support the Senate provided for the regional development bank authorization request last year. We are gravely concerned, however, over the threat of reductions in that authorization bill. Cuts voted in the House consisting of $1.2 billion out of $3.4 billion requested for the Inter-American Development Bank (IDB) and $265 million out of $445 million for the Asian Development Fund (ADF), would have substantial repercussions for the United States. We are pleased that the House-Senate conference has acted to restore these amounts. The conferees have rightly concluded that authorization of the full amounts is critical to the foreign policy and economic interests of the United States. It is vital that this position be sustained when the conferees meet again.

The cuts voted in the House would severely damage U.S. participation in the regional development banks. They would result in an unraveling of the IDB Fifth Replenishment and abrogation of the ADF Second Replenishment, requiring the renegotiation of both agreements.

Under the terms of the ADF replenishment, the United States cannot contribute less than the full amount negotiated; without U.S. participation, the agreement cannot be implemented. The process of renegotiating the agreement would take six months to a year, or longer. Currently, the ADF is out of funds and can only make loan commitments on a contingent basis. As a result, the action taken by the House would effectively eliminate the

Originally presented on March 28, 1980, before the Committee on Foreign Relations of the U.S. Senate.

1980 lending program and could preclude most loans for 1981, as well. This would have a devastating impact on the poorest countries of Asia, which, like Pakistan and Thailand, are also critical to U.S. security interests, because they depend heavily on capital inflows from the ADF to sustain their development efforts.

If the full amount requested for the IDB were not authorized, other donors would in all likelihood call for a renegotiation of the entire replenishment package. Cuts voted by the House would force out over $2 billion in other donor contributions to the replenishment, because the IDB Charter does not permit the U.S. voting power to drop below the current threshold of 34.5 percent. Moreover, given the extremely favorable results of the IDB Fifth Replenishment, from U.S. policy and budgetary perspectives, a renegotiation would not be in the U.S. interest.

As part of the Fifth Replenishment package the United States achieved:

agreement that 50 percent of total Bank lending from this replenishment would directly benefit low-income groups

a lowering of the share of paid-in capital from 10 percent to 7.5 percent (saving the United States $69 million)

a reduction in U.S. annual contributions to the Fund for Special Operations (FSO) from $200 million to $175 million

a substantial increase in the convertible currency contributions of the larger Latin American countries to the FSO

a tripling of the shares of the nonregional members over their initial shares of capital

It is probable that some, maybe all, of these hard fought achievements would be lost in any renegotiation, particularly if the U.S. were to reduce substantially its total contribution. Any renegotiation would take from six months to a year, or longer, given the necessity for parliamentary approval in some member governments. In the meantime, the lending program would come to a halt.

A cessation of lending by the IDB and ADF would have serious adverse repercussions on our national security and foreign policy. Countries and regions of growing importance to U.S. national security, such as Pakistan, Central America, and the Caribbean, would be especially hard hit as a result. Obviously such action would also raise fundamental questions about the reliability of the United States in fulfilling its international commitments and this country's intentions as regards its leadership role in Latin America and Asia.

Authorization of the full amounts in the bill is entirely consistent with current efforts to achieve savings in budgetary outlays during fiscal 1980 and fiscal 1981. Of the $4.0 billion to be authorized, $2.5 billion—more than 60 percent of the total request—is for callable capital subscriptions to the IDB, which are virtually certain never to result in budgetary outlays.

For the $1.5 billion in the request which eventually will result in budgetary outlays, appropriations are being sought over the period fiscal 1980-fiscal 1983. However, the budgetary impact of the drawdown of these funds will be minimal because that drawdown is tied to disbursements required to implement bank projects which take a minimum of five years to complete. We estimate that this bill will result in zero budgetary outlays in fiscal 1980. Budgetary outlays for the total request of $4.0 billion will be less than $7.0 million in fiscal 1981 and less than $33 million in fiscal 1982. Furthermore, as agreed by the conferees, procedures for drawdowns will be changed to delay outlays as long as possible.

For all these reasons, it is essential that the full amounts in last year's authorization request be approved.

## The 1980 Legislation

This year's bill focuses on the poorest countries of the world. IDA recipients include virtually all countries with annual per capita incomes below $320, in addition to scattered countries with slightly higher income levels. Their total population is more than 1.25 billion. The AFDB lends to African countries with incomes averaging $460 per year, and with a total population of 200 million.

There should be no doubt about the overwhelming need among the prospective IDA and AFDB recipients for these programs to be undertaken during the 1980s. Not only do these countries have the lowest per-capita incomes in the world, they have also experienced the slowest economic growth in the post-OPEC era, barely outpacing population growth. On average, over one half of their populations is mired in absolute poverty where hunger, malnutrition, illiteracy, disease, high infant-mortality, and low life-expectancy are an inevitable way of life.

The sum effect of these proposals will be to provide additional lending of over $15 billion during the first half of the decade to the world's very poorest. This means new programs to increase food production and alleviate hunger, to improve health, sanitation, housing, nutrition, and education, to build critical development infrastructure, and to limit burgeoning population growth.

Channelling assistance through the multilateral development banks (MDBs) has the advantage of complying fully with our domestic requirements for budget stringency. United States participation in the MDBs is the most cost-effective approach available to providing substantial amounts of development assistance to the third world. Enormous fiscal advantages derive from our MDB participation because the burden for providing development assistance is shared with other countries, because the MDBs leverage our paid-in contributions through borrowings in world private capital markets, and because the MDBS, through increased purchases of U.S. goods and services, return substantial economic benefits to the U.S. economy—including additional tax receipts which nearly offset U.S. budgetary outlays.

Furthermore, international burden sharing through the banks is becoming more equitably and widely spread. The U.S. share in nearly every MDB in which the United States is currently participating has declined in recent years, while the lending levels of these institutions have increased. Other donor countries now contribute 75 percent of total MDB resources. Moreover, increasing amounts of our contributions are provided via callable capital, not a penny of which has ever left or is likely to ever leave the U.S. Treasury.

Burden sharing, use of callable capital, and the return of economic benefits to the U.S. economy provide a cost-effective combination to reconcile the need for a substantial, viable foreign assistance program with our current requirement for fiscal austerity. Through that combination, for example, the World Bank can now lend approximately $50 for each dollar paid in by the United States at no net cost to the U.S. taxpayer. Although the concessional MDB institutions such as IDA, where there is no callable capital, do not provide this leverage, major cost-effective advantages—through burden sharing and greater tax receipts via expanding U.S. exports—accrue to the United States.

The authorization request for the U.S. share of the Sixth Replenishment of IDA (IDA VI) totals $3.24 billion. The Sixth Replenishment will provide IDA with $12 billion in new resources for lending on concessional terms, over the period fiscal 1981-fiscal 1983, to the world's poorest countries. IDA VI cannot become effective without the participation of the United States.

This bill also would authorize U.S. membership in the African Development Bank, which for the first time will open its doors to nonregional members, thereby broadening the Bank's financial base, enhancing its access to private capital markets, and thus contributing more effectively to Africa's development. In conjunction with nonregional membership, the capital of the AFDB will be increased from $1.5 billion to $6.3 billion to support a lending program for a minimum of five years.

The proposed U.S. subscription to the AFDB would total $359.7 million, or 5.7 percent of the Bank's total capital. This share is sufficient to allow the United States to elect an executive director to the Bank Board.

Twenty-five percent of the U.S. subscription, or $89.9 million, would be paid in. The remainder would take the form of callable capital.

## The Multilateral Development Banks in the 1980s

It is the view of the administration that active, undiminished U.S. support for the multilateral development banks throughout the 1980s will be critical to fundamental U.S. economic, political, and security interests. Those interests include:

### *National Security*

The banks comprise an important part of the international institutional framework which the United States must rely upon to enhance world security. The United States was the principal architect of that framework, and recent events in Southwest Asia have demonstrated its importance to a secure, stable world environment. United States security interests are so far-reaching that defense of those interests would be unthinkable without relying upon the multilateral process through the existing institutional framework. The responses of the United States to the crises in Iran and Afghanistan, and the results of those collective, collaborative efforts with much of the developing world, have demonstrated the importance of the multilateral process in promoting our foreign policy and national security interests. The United States must therefore give its fullest support to the process in order to keep it working to support U.S. interests.

In support of collective security action, the banks are critical to the maintenance of political stability in each of the major regions of the world and in key countries. One need only scan the list of the largest MDB borrowers—Mexico, Brazil, India, Korea, Pakistan, Egypt, Indonesia, Colombia, Yugoslavia, Kenya, and Turkey—to grasp the importance of the MDBs to U.S. security by way of their contributions to growth and material well-being, and thus to political stability in key regions of the world.

Finally, there is the growing importance of U.S. dependence on critical raw materials from the developing world. The United States is nearly totally dependent upon the developing countries for supplies of bauxite, tin, manganese, and natural rubber, as well as certain food-stuffs. The United States and the rest of the Western World have a vital stake in promoting the stability and growth of the economies of developing countries which produce critical new materials and in retaining access to these supplies.

*The Health of the International Economic System*

In 1979, MDB loan commitments totalled nearly $14 billion. This represents by far the largest official source of external capital for the developing world. As such, the MDBs contribute in a major way to economic growth and stability in recipient developing countries and in rapidly expanding trade between the third world and the developed countries. In providing dispassionate policy advice, in preparing development projects based upon objective economic criteria, and in insisting upon rational economic policies within recipient countries, the MDBs are an important, respected force for the maintenance of an efficient, responsive international market economy. The impact of the banks in this regard, and their resulting contribution to the health and resilience of the world economy, is often overlooked but cannot be overstated.

Another intangible is the inducement of the banks to cooperative efforts among developed and developing countries, where relations in the recent past have too often been characterized by confrontation and hostility to resolve pressing international economic problems. Cooperation here means developed and developing countries working together to focus bank policies and resources to respond to critical world needs. Most recently, this has meant both shifting MDB lending away from traditional infrastructure to agriculture and rural development to more directly benefit the poor and to increase food production and greatly expanding lending to increase developing country energy production.

The banks also contribute to the effort to recycle funds from the oil-producing countries to the developing world. Recent oil price increases will add about $14 billion to the current account deficits, totaling approximately $50 billion, for the oil-importing developing countries this year. Though the basic objective of bank loans is to promote long-run development in recipient countries, their role in this regard will become more prominent and vital to the world economy in the 1980s.

*Direct U.S. Economic Benefits*

The most rapidly growing developing countries, which, not coincidentally, are among the largest MDB borrowers, are also the most rapidly growing export markets for the United States. Generally, nonoil developing countries account for about 25 percent of U.S. exports, including one-quarter of U.S. manufactured exports. These markets have become more important to U.S. trade than the entire European Community.

Through the contributions of other MDB donors, which on average comprise 75 percent of the total, and through the use of callable capital,

MDB loans result in expenditures on U.S. goods and services well in excess of U.S. contributions to the banks. From the inception of the banks through 1978, the cumulative current account surplus for the United States directly attributable to MDB activities (the purchase of U.S. goods and services, net interest payments to U.S. MDB bondholders, and MDB administrative expenses in the United States) has been \$11 billion. Cumulative U.S. paid-in contributions to the banks, by comparison, totaled \$7 billion. This means that every dollar contributed to the MDBs results in \$1.57 being injected directly into the U.S. economy.

The total economic effects, however, are much larger and more broadly based than the effects directly observable from our balance of payments. That \$1.57 becomes the income of a U.S. exporter, bondholder, or Bank employee residing in the United States. It is in turn respent, resulting in multiple increases in U.S. national income, employment, and federal government and local tax receipts.

Treasury analysis shows that over the period 1977-1978 every dollar contributed to the MDBs has resulted in an increase of U.S. GNP of \$3.00. This 3-for-1 multiplier effect is sizable and stems, in part, from the unique characteristics of the MDBs, that is, their multilateral character, which provides for other donor country contributions, and the availability of callable capital, which permits substantial borrowing on private capital markets. Total U.S. GNP growth directly attributable to MDB activities averaged \$2.7 billion over 1977-1978, raising net federal tax receipts by \$720 million annually and reducing the net cost to the federal budget for our participation in the banks to \$170 million each year. If increased local tax receipts were included, the net cost to the American taxpayer probably would be minimal.

## Developing Country Prospects for the 1980s

The record for the developing countries over the past two decades, which spans the work of the MDBs including IDA, shows clear progress. During the decade of the 1960s and up to the 1974 surge in OPEC oil prices, gross domestic product for the developing countries grew at 6 percent or more annually, exceeding growth in the industrialized countries. Developing countries' exports of manufactured goods grew at nearly 13 percent annually, and their share of total world manufactured exports grew from 6 percent to 10 percent during that period.

Moreover, each of the quality-of-life standards—life expectancy, infant mortality, literacy, access to potable water, and calories as a percent of daily requirements—showed significant improvements during the 1960s and 1970s and a narrowing of the gap with the industrialized countries. Average per capita income for the developing countries also has approximately doubled in real terms since 1960.

Despite recent progress in many areas, the prospects for the developing countries in the 1980s are not optimistic. In part this is because the world economy has moved haltingly, at best, to recover from the oil price increases and subsequent recession of the mid-1970s and because the recovery remains far from complete. Thus, for the 1970s, while the per capita GNP of the major oil-exporting countries grew at 6.6 percent per annum, per capita income grew at 3.6 percent for the middle-income developing countries and fell off to only 1.7 percent per year for the poorest developing countries. For the poorest countries in Africa per capita growth was an imperceptible 0.2 percent.

In large part these meager results reflect a general slow-down in growth throughout the developing world in the 1974-1979 period. The causes of that slow-down—surging oil prices, worldwide inflation, slower growth in the industrialized countries, and declining real supplies of external capital—cast long shadows over prospects for the 1980s.

Under the most optimistic assumptions of vigorous economic growth in developing countries in the 1980s, the World Bank has projected that their per capita income will increase 4.2 percent per annum. However, per capita income would increase by only 3.5 percent in the poorest developing countries and under 2 percent in Sub-Saharan Africa. Under more realistic assumptions, the per capita income of the developing countries can be expected to increase at an average rate of between 2.4 percent and 3.3 percent but at only 1 percent or less in the poorest countries of Africa and under 3 percent in the low-income Asian countries.

Hence, per capita income in the poorest developing countries, with 1.25 billion people, will probably increase only $1-10 per year over the next decade. The World Bank also estimates that, realistically, we can only expect to reduce the numbers of people living in absolute poverty—that bare survival state conditioned by malnutrition, illiteracy, disease, high infant mortality, and low life expectancy—from 800 million to 600 million by the end of the century.

Equally disturbing is the fact that, while developing country food production is barely keeping abreast of overall population growth, in the poorest developing countries population growth at 2.4 percent a year has been outpacing food production, which has grown at less than one percent annually since 1961. The combined effects of poverty and food insecurity, neither of which is being ameliorated in the poorest countries, are interacting to cause a worsening problem of hunger. Millions of people—more than three-quarters of whom live on the Indian subcontinent, in Southeast Asia, and in Sub-Saharan Africa—are afflicted by hunger. Short of a massive effort at increasing food production in the poorest developing countries themselves, this condition will remain widespread throughout the 1980s.

### The Role of the Multilateral Development Banks and U.S. Objectives in the 1980s

These somber prospects have led us to conclude that the multilateral development banks must play a major worldwide development role in the 1980s. The MDBs have the technical expertise and the experience to use the capital resources which we propose to provide them for the coming years. Moreover, they do so in an extremely cost-effective manner through the sharing of the burden of foreign assistance with other donor countries and long-term borrowing on capital markets with the backing of callable capital, at minimum cost to the U.S. taxpayer.

The MDBs are the most efficient, effective instruments to pursue broad-based development strategies in the developing world. At the microeconomic level, they follow detailed and rigorous loan appraisal processes to ensure that every dollar of development lending yields maximum benefits. Loan analysis is performed solely on the basis of relevant economic and technical considerations. Their apolitical nature also carries with it a special trust which enables the staffs of MDBs to influence strongly borrowing countries in the adoption of sound policies.

The United States also has significant policy leverage in the banks relative to both the proportion and dollar amounts of its contributions. Over the recent past, the United States has pursued a number of policy objectives in the MDBs to promote further their objective of helping the developing countries attain higher standards of material well-being and to help alleviate the conditions of absolute poverty. Among these objectives have been to reach the poor more effectively and efficiently, to increase food production substantially, and to increase both the amounts and proportion of lending for projects designed to increase world energy supplies.

In response to U.S. urging, all the MDBs have redirected the sectoral composition of their lending to better meet basic human needs and to ensure that proportionally more project benefits flow to lower-income groups in borrowing countries. This redirection is reflected in the rapid growth of lending for agricultural projects.

World Bank Group lending for agriculture, one-third of which is coming from IDA, has increased 145 percent in the past five years. For IDA alone, loans for the agricultural sector have grown by 427 percent. During that period, IBRD/IDA activities have provided the base for producing one-third of all increased fertilizer production in the developing countries for the first half of the 1980s, one-fifth of the total investment in rural road networks in developing countries, and one-quarter of total public investment in developing country irrigation systems. Furthermore, 358 IBRD/IDA agricultural projects over these past five years have had the rural poor as their principal beneficiaries, and an estimated 60 million of the 100 million direct beneficiaries of these projects had incomes below the absolute poverty levels in their respective countries.

Currently, approximately 46 percent and 30 percent of IDA and IBRD lending, respectively, flows to the agricultural sector, up from 37 percent and 11 percent respectively in the early 1970s. Over 75 percent of combined IBRD/IDA agricultural assistance is now directed toward expanding food production. As noted in the forthcoming report of the President's Commission of World Hunger, the World Bank Group is the world's largest single source of external funding for developing world agriculture. The World Bank expects to finance projects which will contribute up to 20 percent of the increase in annual food production in its developing member countries in the 1980s. It is due to this effort that the President's Commission on World Hunger has concluded that the United States should strongly support the activities of the MDBs, including an increase in U.S. contributions to the concessional windows of the banks.

An important means to implement the objective of more effectively and directly reaching the poor has been to encourage greater utilization of capital-saving technologies. Such technologies have the advantage of increasing the productivity and incomes of poor people at low per capita costs by insuring that the maximum numbers of people benefit from MDB projects and by promoting the most efficient use of factor availabilities. The United States has sought greater utilization and development of capital-saving technologies in the MDBs by encouraging policy decisions in the banks, urging increased MDB staff focus on the appropriateness of technologies, and constantly reviewing project loans to assure improved application.

The United States has also been at the forefront in urging the MDBs to adopt a comprehensive energy program. In the World Bank Group in January 1979, the Board of Executive Directors approved an expansion of the IBRD/IDA energy program. That program is now planned to grow to at least 15 percent of total Bank lending within five years.

Over the 1980-1984 period, the World Bank Group will lend $7.7 billion for the exploration, production, and development of oil, gas, and coal and for the construction of new hydroelectric facilities. The loans will be combined with approximately three times as much private and government financing. When the projects are in operation, they will produce additional primary energy fuel in oil-importing developing countries estimated to equal between 2 and 2.5 million barrels a day of oil. This should help to increase world supply and thereby reduce pressures on world oil prices, as well as deal directly with one of the most critical bottlenecks to development.

## The International Development Association

The International Development Association (IDA) is central to the attack on poverty in the poorest countries in the world. The record of that institution demonstrates clearly that developed and developing countries can work successfully to resolve common problems. Rhetoric and confrontation have no part to play in IDA programs. IDA recipients have come to appreciate and depend upon concrete development projects and programs which are designed to resolve real economic problems and to produce material improvement in the lives of their people.

It is important that the United States strongly support cooperative programs for mutual gain such as IDA. It serves to undermine those in the developing world who favor confrontation with the United States, to preempt proposals in North-South fora which are adverse to U.S. economic and politcal interests, and to enhance prospects for developing country support on issues of primary importance to the United States. At a time when global economic difficulties are exposing nearly all the poorer developing countries to serious threats of political, economic, and social instability, IDA is making an invaluable contribution to our national security and other U.S. foreign policy objectives, via the multilateral process.

The rather bleak prospects for the low-income countries of Africa and Asia give IDA a vital development role to play in the 1980s. IDA is the largest source of concessional resources in the world, the largest source of external financing for the countries of Africa, and the centerpiece of multilateral efforts to utilize concessional resources effectively within broad-based development strategies. As such, it will be the major hope for the poorest developing countries and their 1.25 billion people over the next decade.

IDA will be crucial in determining whether per capita food production in the poorest LDCs will increase and whether real progress is made in alleviating world hunger. Nearly two-thirds of the external financing requirements of the low-income developing countries will need to be met through disbursements of concessional capital, of which IDA will be the largest single source, during the last half of the 1980s. IDA will be key in determining whether the more than 800 million persons mired in absolute poverty can be significantly reduced by the end of this century. It will depend largly upon IDA as to whether the poorest developing countries will be able to undertake programs to improve education, health, sanitation, housing, nutrition, and population control throughout the 1980s.

About 90 percent of IDA lending goes to countries with annual per capital incomes below $320 (1978 dollars). None of IDA's recipients has a per capita income above $625. The 54 current IDA borrowers account for approximately 31 percent of the world's population but only 3 percent of global gross national product. Average life expectancy in these countries is about fifty years, the adult literacy rate is 36 percent, and the labor force is expanding at 2 percent per year. Most of these countries are in South Asia and in Sub-Saharan Africa, two regions which borrowed 80 percent of IDA resouces in fiscal 1979. IDA's lending policy also focuses on development projects which reach the lowest 40 percent of the income earners within the recipient borrowing countries.

All IDA credits to date have been for a term of fifty years. After a ten-year period of grace, one percent of the credit is repaid annually for ten years, while in the remaining thirty years 3 percent is repaid annually. There is an annual service charge of 0.75 percent on the disbursed portion of each credit to cover administrative costs. All credits are repayable in convertible currency.

During nineteen years of operations through June 30, 1979, IDA has made development credits aggregating $16.7 billion to seventy-four countries. There has never been a default on an IDA loan by any borrower.

**IDA VI Replenishment**

A major step in assuring that IDA will be adequately financed to carry out its current task in the 1980s is the agreement which has been reached on a $12 billion replenishment of IDA for lending over the years fiscal 1981 through fiscal 1983. The proposed Sixth Replenishment will enable IDA to expand its lending from an average of $3 billion per year during IDA V, to $3.5 billion in fiscal 1981, $4.0 billion in fiscal 1982, and $4.5 billion in fiscal 1983. The $12 billion IDA VI replenishment represents a real increase of only 4.5 percent over IDA V, the minimum considered necessary to spur additional growth in the poorest developing countries. The increase in IDA VI is far below those of previous IDA replenishments.

It must be noted that IDA VI cannot become effective without full U.S. participation. Unless additional funds become available, the Association will exhaust its commitment authority by June 30, 1980, with drastic consequences for the poorest, most populous countries of the world.

The IDA VI negotiations were protracted and difficult. On the one hand, it was widely recognized that the needs of the poorest developing countries are immense and growing and that growth among a number of the countries had been stagnating in recent years. As a result, the World Bank originally proposed a replenishment of $15 billion. On the other hand, a number of donors, including the United States, faced severe budgetary constraints. These opposing views eventually reached a compromise agreement for a $12 billion replenishment despite the views of a number of donors that the urgency of the poverty problem among the poorest developing countries demanded a larger replenishment package. Nevertheless, the agreement reached will permit a 4-5 percent annual real growth in IDA lending over the period of fiscal 1981-fiscal 1983.

The U.S. share of IDA VI will be 27 percent, sharply lower than the 31.04 percent U.S. share of IDA V. The U.S. decline will enable the level of the U.S. contribution to show no real growth relative to IDA V—total lending will rise 4-5 percent while the U.S. share declines by 4 percent. The U.S. share will total $3.24 billion, or an annual U.S. contribution of $1.08 million. The full U.S. contribution must be authorized. Otherwise the United States could not participate in the replenishment, and IDA VI, which took more than a year to achieve, would have to be renegotiated. In the interim IDA lending would cease.

It was through improved burdensharing in IDA VI that a modest real increase in IDA's development resources will be achieved. The large reduction in the U.S. share was offset by substantial increases in the shares of Germany (from 10.9 percent to 12.5 percent) and especially Japan (from 10.3 percent to 14.7 percent). For the first time in an IDA replenishment the combined shares of these two countries will exceed that of the United States. Six members, mostly developing countries including Mexico, Argentina, and Brazil, will provide IDA with resources for the first time. These burden-sharing achievements were explicit negotiating objectives of the United States under the mandate of the Congress to reduce significantly the U.S. share in IDA.

Other negotiating accomplishments included agreement that:

> Energy lending would expand rapidly during IDA VI, thus increasing world supplies and helping to ease upward price pressure.
>
> IDA's major thrust would continue to be in reaching the poor. The proportion of IDA lending to agriculture and rural development would expand through fiscal 1983. Lending for the urban poor would also increase.
>
> Supervision and evaluation of IDA projects would be stepped up using standards and procedures set out in detail during the negotiations, thereby enhancing the operating efficiency of what is universally recognized as a superbly run institution.

Replenishment of IDA, as agreed in these negotiations, is essential if the poorest developing countries are to have any prospect of achieving meaningful growth in the 1980s. IDA VI is also necessary if we are to move toward alleviating world hunger and reducing absolute poverty during the decade. It will make an important contribution toward meeting worldwide energy needs in the coming years. Finally, the continued strong presence of

IDA throughout the poorest regions of the third world will be critical to the maintenance of political and economic stability and ultimately peace. We could pay a heavy price by its absence. United States national interest dictates that we fully support this replenishment of IDA.

**United States Membership in the African Development Bank**

Development performance in Africa throughout the 1970s has been particularly disappointing. For the poorest countries—the bulk of the countries in Sub-Saharan Africa—per capita income growth for the decade averaged 0.2 percent per year. This means that throughout the 1970s much of the population of Sub-Saharan Africa increased their incomes by less than $1 per year. The "middle-income" countries of Sub-Saharan Africa with an average annual per capital income of $460 fared little better. Per capita income for these countries increased at 1.4 percent per year, the lowest growth rate of any region of the world, including the poorest, most populous countries of Asia.

Furthermore, prospects are that per capita income growth will continue to either stagnate or improve imperceptibly throughout the decade of the 1980s. The World Bank projects an annual increase of between 0.7 and 1.9 percent for the poorest African countries and between 0.7 and 2.2 percent for the middle-income countries, depending upon low- or high-growth assumptions.

Even such per capita income growth notions fail to reflect the immense development problems facing the developing countries of Africa in the 1980s. These countries have the lowest literacy rates, the lowest life expectancies, the highest population growth rates, and the largest percentage of people living in absolute poverty of any major developing region on the globe. This is somewhat ironic given that Africa is perhaps the richest of the developing country continents in natural resources—with large sources of bauxite, oil, potential hydroelectric power, manganese, copper, precious minerals, and vast potential for agricultural production.

It is concern over the development prospects for the countries of Africa, our common cultural heritage with the Sub-Saharan countries, and the longstanding policy of this administration to expand and strengthen U.S. ties with Africa that has resulted in our proposing U.S. membership in the African Development Bank (AFDB).

The AFDB was established in 1964, to lend at near-market terms for the economic and social development of its African members and to promote regional cooperation. To meet the challenge of Africa's poverty, loans are provided primarily to strengthen the agricultural sector and to finance critically needed infrastructure. The AFDB's lending activities are financed through member country paid-in capital subscriptions and borrowings in international capital markets.

While the United States and other nonregional countries are members of the AFDB's concessional loan affiliate, the African Development Fund, membership in the Bank to date has been restricted to African nations. The limited capital resources of its African members have severely restricted the AFDB's lending program and its access to private capital markets.

Consequently, in May 1979, the governors of the AFDB invited nonregional countries to joint their institution. Nonregional membership will expand and diversify the Bank's financial base and greatly enhance its access to private capital markets. As a result, the Bank will be able to increase its lending program substantially over the next five years and contribute more effectively to development of the continent.

### Results of the AFDB Negotiations

Active U.S. participation in the nonregional membership negotiations and support for U.S. membership in the AFDB were based on numerous U.S. interests which Bank membership would serve. The United States has rapidly expanding economic and political interests in Africa which would be furthered by supporting the continent's development through the AFDB. In addition, United States membership in the African Development Bank was seen as another means to concentrate increasing development assistance on the poor. Most of the countries which are middle-income for Africa—and thus receive nonconcessional AFDB loans—are at a level of development far below that of the middle-income countries of other regions. The middle-income countries of Sub-Saharan Africa have an average per capita income of $460 compared to $990 in other developing regions.

The multilateral character of the AFDB would provide a firm basis for sharing the cost of Africa's development with other countries. In the 1960s, the United States had already entered into similar multilateral partnerships with the nations of Latin America and Asia through the Inter-American Development Bank and the Asian Development Bank. Participation in the AFDB would complete this series of partnerships in an established and recognized pan-African institution.

In addition, by financing the basic infrastructure needs of African countries (roads, power, water supply, and sewerage) and agricultural projects, the Bank would complement increasing U.S. bilateral assistance efforts in Africa which focus more on meeting basic human needs. The AFDB would also complement IDA's activities by directing two-thirds of its lending to African countries with annual per capita incomes between $320 and

$700, while IDA concentrates its resources on those African nations with less than $320 per capita.

In conjunction with the entry of nonregional members the capital of the Bank will be increased from about $1.5 billion to $6.3 billion, over a five-year period. Of this increase, the regional members would provide 57 percent or $2.8 billion. The twenty-one nonregional countries seeking membership—the countries of Western Europe, Canada, Japan, Korea, Yugoslavia, and Kuwait as well as the United States—would subscribe $2.1 billion. Twenty-five percent of the increase, or $1.2 billion, will be paid-in capital with the remaining 75 percent ($3.6 billion) in callable capital.

The proposed U.S. subscription would total $360 million—5.7 percent of the Bank's total capital and 17 percent of the nonregional share. The U.S. nonregional share is equivalent to the U.S. share of the current replenishment of the African Development Fund. This share represents an effort to balance our interest in increased burden sharing with other donor countries with our desire to become more actively involved in the economic and social development of Africa.

In order to accommodate adequate representation on the Board of Directors by the nonregional countries, the Board will be expanded from the current nine to eighteen members. Twelve directors will be elected by the regional members and six by the nonregional members, reflecting the proportional participation of each group in the capital stock of the AFDB. The size of the proposed U.S. share of AFDB capital will enable the United States to elect an American as director to the Bank's Board.

United States membership in the AFDB comes at an opportune time. It is fitting that the United States should join a major pan-African institution, as the largest nonregional member, during a period when our overall relations with the nations of Africa have experienced dramatic improvement. The Sub-Saharan region remains politically volatile and the rapid expansion of the AFDB will help to stabilize the region by strengthening the healthier independent African nations, promoting pan-African cooperation, and assisting the region to evolve peacefully toward full political autonomy.

Finally, recent poor growth performance of the middle-income African countries and cloudy prospects for the 1980s show the necessity for a sizeable expansion of the African Bank's lending program. These countries have a critical need to diversify their economies: low growth projections for the 1980s are due, in large part, to high share of slow-growing primary products in their exports which will limit overall export expansion. Furthermore, many of these countries, including Kenya, Ivory Coast, Morocco, Nigeria, and Gabon, among others, have demonstrated rapid development potential and the capability of absorbing capital resources efficiently.

## Treatment of U.S. Subscriptions to IBRD and ADB Callable Capital

The administration is also proposing amendments to those legislative provisions enacted by the Congress in 1977 which require that full appropriations be obtained prior to U.S. subscriptions to the Selective Capital Increase of the IBRD and the Second Capital Increase of the ADB. Under the proposed amendments, subscriptions to IBRD and ADB callable capital stock could be made after program limitations on the subscriptions are enacted in the Foreign Assistance Appropriations Act, rather than actual appropriations.

The proposed amendments would make consistent the statutory terms under which the United States can subscribe to IBRD and ADB callable capital stock with the terms provided in the authorizing legislation for the proposed replenishment of the IDB, as well as with the provisions in the bill for initial subscriptions to the capital stock of the AFDB. The amendments are essential to allow implementation of the president's fiscal 1981 budget, which proposes enactment of program limitations in the fiscal 1981 Foreign Assistance Appropriations Act for U.S. subscriptions to callable capital stock in the MDBs, including the IBRD and ADB.

The change in the treatment of callable capital is being proposed because the appropriation for the full amount of callable capital and the resulting scoring of the appropriated amounts as budget authority distort the true size of the request for the MDBs.

The budgetary and appropriations treatment of callable capital is an issue that has been under intense consideration for over a year both within the administration and between the administration and Congress. Changing the treatment of callable capital was discussed last year during consideration of S. 662. At that time, the Committee approved language which authorized U.S. subscriptions to callable capital of the Inter-American Development Bank without requiring prior appropriations to fund these subscriptions.

The "callable capital" concept is one of the most attractive features of the multilateral development banks and results in considerable budgetary savings for the U.S. government. With callable capital as backing, the MDBs are able to borrow most of the nonconcessional funds they require in international capital markets. The cost to the U.S. government of subscriptions to callable capital is solely contingent in nature, since callable capital can only be used to meet obligations of the MDBs for funds borrowed or guaranteed by them in the unlikely event that the banks' other resources are insufficient to meet those liabilities.

The risk of a "call" is extremely slight. The loan portfolios of the

MDBs are distributed broadly, and major defaults are unlikely. Even if a number of their largest borrowers were to default, the MDBs have very considerable financial assets upon which they could draw. Moreover, prior subscriptions to individual MDBs totaling $11.5 billion have been funded by the Congress against potential U.S. liabilities, of which $8.4 billion relates to U.S. subscriptions to IBRD and ADB callable capital, the two institutions for which amendments are being proposed. In the IBRD, all prior U.S. subscriptions to callable capital have been fully funded. In the ADB, of the $736 million in U.S. subscriptions to callable capital, all but $126 million has been appropriated.

It is therefore virtually certain that there will never be budget outlays resulting from U.S. subscriptions affected by these amendments. Thus, as in other donor countries, we propose to cease treating callable capital subscriptions as though they would have an outlay impact, when that is not the case.

## Conclusion

There is a very real need for continued growth in IDA lending and for a strengthening and expansion of the African Development Bank's activities in the 1980s, as provided in this bill. Together, these proposals will act to improve materially the lives of one and a half billion of the world's poorest people, residing in the world's poorest countries.

The Sixth Replenishment of IDA is essential if the poorest countries, in the 1980s, are to increase per capita income levels meaningfully, reduce the numbers of people living in absolute poverty, make progress toward alleviating world hunger, continue to narrow the gap with the middle-income and developed countries in life expectancy, literacy, and infant mortality, build the basic infrastructure required for development, and meet their energy needs.

United States membership in the AFDB and expansion of that institution's capital base are required to promote economic progress in Africa, expand U.S. economic and political interests there, and solidify recent improvements in U.S. relations with a large number of African nations.

Continued emphasis on the MDBs to channel an increasing proportion of U.S. development assistance is fully consistent with our domestic concerns over cost-effectiveness and fiscal austerity. The MDBs allow us to reconcile the overwhelming need for a viable development assistance program throughout the 1980s with the pursuit of a tough domestic anti-inflation program, because they provide enormous fiscal advantages. These include burden sharing of development assistance with other countries, the leveraging of U.S. contribution through borrowings in world capital markets, and purchases of U.S. goods and services which return substantial economic benefits including increased tax receipts which nearly offset U.S. budgetary outlays for our participation in the banks.

I strongly urge your support for U.S. participation in the Sixth Replenishment of the International Development Association, for U.S. membership in the African Development Bank, and for changes in the budgetary and appropriations treatment of U.S. subscriptions to the World Bank and Asian Development Bank callable capital.

# 12 The Economic Interests of the United States and Saudi Arabia

There are few areas in the world where as many compelling American interests intersect as in the Middle East. With each passing month, the region seems to take on increasing significance. I would like to focus my remarks on one country in this critical area—Saudi Arabia.

Three years ago during Crown Prince Fahd's visit to the United States, President Carter said, "I think it is accurate to say that the future of Saudi Arabia and the future of the United States are tied together very closely in an irrevocable way. It is very valuable to us to understand, to preserve, and to strengthen this important friendship."

There are many important aspects to the United States—Saudi relationship. Energy and finance are key elements, with considerable impact not only on our own economies but on the entire world. Trade in nonenergy products is becoming increasingly important, as well. The United States-Saudi Joint Economic Commission offers a third facet of our economic relations which is important to Saudi economic development and our continued close cooperation in the future.

I would like to touch on our mutual interests in energy, finance and trade, and then discuss in some detail about the ongoing work of the Joint Commission.

## Energy/Finance

Oil is the historic basis of the United States-Saudi Arabian friendship. Saudi Arabia's supplies of energy are crucial to the United States and world economies. Without sufficient petroleum at reasonable prices, stable noninflationary growth becomes very difficult to achieve. Saudi Arabia is now the leading supplier of oil to the United States accounting for almost 20 percent of our imports. It also accounts for 19 percent of free world crude oil production.

The United States and Saudi Arabia have mutual interests in three key areas: investments, energy conservation, and the security of oil supplies. First, because its oil income has exceeded its revenue needs, Saudi Arabia has accumulated substantial financial resources for which it has sought ap-

Originally presented on March 18, 1980, before the American Arab Association for Commerce and Industry in New York City.

propriate investment opportunities. The United States has been and continues to be the single largest recipient of Saudi investments. Most of Saudi Arabia's non-U.S. investments are also dollar denominated. The strength of the dollar thus depends importantly on Saudi management of their surpluses. In turn, the value of Saudi investments depends on a strong and stable dollar.

A second interdependence relates to Saudi oil production and U.S. energy consumption. Since Saudi Arabia would prefer to limit oil production, it is interested in implementation of a U.S. energy program which emphasizes both conservation and the development of alternate energy resources. Saudi spokesmen in fact have linked price moderation on their part to conservation on our part.

Third, as the world's largest oil supplier, Saudi Arabia's security is vital to the United States and other consumers. Any disruption to Saudi oil supplies would have major adverse effects on us, as well as on Saudi Arabia itself.

These issues are intimately linked but I believe oil supplies and price, petrodollars, and the dollar are of most interest to this group.

**Oil Supply and Price**

On the supply side, Saudi Arabia has the world's largest proved reserves of petroleum (roughly 20 percent of the world's total) and possesses the capacity to become the world's largest oil producer. In the past, it has clearly been the dominant force within OPEC. While the sheer size of its oil reserves and production are important, a major source of its political power within OPEC has been its ability to vary oil production over a very wide range. Because of its lower revenue needs relative to its export earnings, it was able to reduce production to avoid intra-OPEC competition for market shares at times when supplies were slack. On the other hand, because of its considerable excess production capacity, it was capable of increasing its supplies to the oil market if other producers sought to raise prices above levels it believed appropriate.

The results of the Iranian crisis and the Caracus meeting last December are clear indications, however, that at least one of the major conditions for Saudi price leadership within OPEC is disappearing. With very little spare capacity available, Saudi Arabia has been less influential than in the past in moderating OPEC pricing decisions. Similarly, it was not able to fill the gap in supply caused by the loss of 4.5 to 5.0 million barrels per day (mmb/d) of Iranian exports in the early part of 1979.

Nevertheless, Saudi Arabia has played a most helpful role during the last year. For example, it increased production in late 1978 to the maximum sustainable capacity of over 10 mmb/d, and to 9.5 mmb/d during four of the last five quarters—the latter being 1 mmb/d above the normal Saudi production ceiling. Similarly, on the price side, Saudi Arabia alone is charging the lowest price, $26 per barrel, for its Arabian light crude, the traditional OPEC benchmark. We hope that Saudi Arabia will continue to display this strong sense of reasonableness toward the international economy with respect to both oil supply and price.

We assume the Saudis will be considering substantial investments in new productive capacity if they are to continue to play a restraining role within OPEC. Saudi intentions in this area are not completely clear, but on a sustainable basis their current target appears to be 12 mmb/d. The main obstacle has been self-imposed investment constraints. Saudi Arabia is requiring that all investment by Aramco to maintain or expand productive capacity be derived from internally generated funds. Before the recent price increases, it appeared that this would delay attainment of the 12 mmb/d target, but the additional revenues now foreseen may change this situation. In any event, the year 1984 has recently been mentioned by several Saudi spokesmen for attainment of this target.

The Saudis can be expected to take a number of considerations into account in deciding how to implement the present target and whether to expand the target further. Some of these are political, but a number are economic:

> Substantial investment funds are required merely to maintain existing capacity, as is the case with any aging oil fields;
>
> Additional investments would be required to expand capacity;
>
> The Saudis are giving high priority to other investments: refining, petrochemicals, modernization more broadly;
>
> There is growing concern in Saudi Arabia about producing oil at levels in excess of current income needs;
>
> Many also argue that oil in the ground is a better investment than financial assets abroad.

The situation, thus, is as follows:

> The Saudis have played a constructive leadership role in OPEC. They have normally attempted to moderate OPEC price increases and help assure the supplies needed for world economic health.
>
> Continuation of a Saudi leadership role requires substantial investments so as to create sufficient excess capacity.

> Some Saudis are doubtful that this is in their interest, particularly since they have seen consuming countries like the United States as slow to take the steps necessary to conserve oil use.
>
> The Saudi position to date, however, has recognized that Saudi production levels must take into account the economic health and political stability of the free world.

There is much the United States and other oil consuming nations can do to sustain this sense of international responsibility. It is also important to continue the bilateral dialogue which to date has been profitable to both countries and to attempt to find a resolution of any real differences between us.

**Saudi Investments**

The other side of the coin to expanding Saudi oil production—above that needed for its own internal development—is the need for attractive investment opportunities.

Saudi Arabia has run large current account surpluses, totaling almost $80 billion since 1974. The size of the surplus has declined since the extraordinary $23 billion in 1974, as Saudi Arabia's ambitious development program has taken hold. However, the recent oil price increases have lead to a reversal of this trend. We expect Saudi Arabia to run substantial surpluses in the near term.

The Saudi Arabian government has been most explicit in detailing the approach it takes toward investments. The Saudis have stated that they seek to play a constructive role, recognizing the need to act with larger issues in mind than solely their own profit. In this regard, they have avoided speculative transactions and investment in such sensitive areas as real estate or controlling interests in U.S. firms. According to Governor Quraishi, head of the Saudi Arabian Monetary Agency, their investment managers in this country have been instructed that at no time may Saudi investments reach 5 percent of the voting stock of any company. He has further indicated that their holdings of U.S. government securities constitute the largest single component of their international reserves.

It is also evident that Saudi Arabia views its investments as crucial for its future and believes they will have to be increasingly employed to finance domestic development as oil reserves decline. Accordingly, the Saudis have followed a conservative investment policy with emphasis on income, security, and liquidity.

Fulfillment of such a policy is not an easy task, however. Very few markets offer the Saudis sufficient liquidity and choice of investment opportunities, combined with minimal sovereign, exchange rate, and convertibility risks. The U.S. capital market, and the closely related Eurodollar market, are easily the largest, broadest, most liquid, and most accessible. Thus, it is not surprising that Saudi Arabia has chosen to invest around 85 percent of its funds in the United States and in deposits in the Eurobanking market, the bulk of which are in dollars. We hope it will continue to do so.

## U.S. Energy/Inflation Programs

From its own perspective, Saudi Arabia clearly has a keen interest in U.S. domestic policy efforts to develop a comprehensive energy program and to effectively fight inflation. The United States has recently taken a number of steps toward comprehensive programs in both of these key areas. I would like to discuss them briefly.

In the energy area, the President's decision to decontrol domestic oil prices was a critically important step, complemented by the numerous other measures we have taken to cut domestic demand: mandatory automobile mileage standards, mandatory thermostat settings, switching from oil to gas, savings in federal government operations, changed environmental regulations, and appeals to voluntary conservation. The President has established ceilings for net oil imports of 8.2 mmb/d in 1979 and 1980—300,000 below the actual 1978 level—and has indicated he is prepared to lower this ceiling further if other oil-consuming countries will join in mutual reductions.

To stimulate production of alternatives to imported oil from our domestic energy resources, the President has proposed a Synthetic Fuels Corporation to encourage the production of synthetic fuels. He has proposed the creation of an Energy Mobilization Board to minimize delays in reviews of the construction of energy projects of major national interest, consistent with safeguarding the environment. The House of Representatives has passed a windfall profits tax which will provide additional funds for developing alternative energy sources, a similar bill has now gone to the Senate floor.

Finally, new targets have been established for nationwide gasoline consumption through agreement with the state governors. This will result in savings of about 400,000 gallons per day, roughly a 5.5 percent decrease from average U.S. daily consumption in 1979. Last Friday the President also announced the imposition of a gasoline conservation fee on imported oil of $4.62 per barrel, which will be applied solely to gasoline in an amount equal to about 10 cents a gallon. This should reduce U.S. gasoline consumption by 100,000 barrels per day after one year. The President also will send to Congress legislation establishing a motor fuels tax designed to replace this gasoline conservation fee.

These measures represent a strong U.S. effort to achieve a comprehensive energy program to both increase domestic energy production and curb U.S. energy consumption, in recognition of our own responsibilities in this key area.

Last Friday the President also announced a major new anti-inflation program. In addition to the energy conservation measures I have already summarized, this program includes:

1. Stringent efforts to achieve a balanced budget in fiscal 1981 through reductions in virtually every area of the budget not essential to our national security; direct expenditure cuts for government personnel, operations, and maintenance; a freeze in federal civilian employment, aiming at an overall reduction of 20,000 employees by the end of 1980; a reduction in ongoing spending programs; increased Defense Department efficiencies to offset a large part of its cost increases; intensified pay and price monitoring; and proposed legislation to permit withholding of taxes on interest and dividend payments;

2. Authorization for new restraints on the growth of credit including consumer loans; restraint on large nonmember banks and money market mutual funds; voluntary restraint on excessive growth in loans by large banks and other lenders; a surcharge of 3 percent on borrowing by large banks at the discount window; and a $4 billion cut in federal loans and loan guarantees in fiscal 1981;

3. Long-term economic structural changes including renewed appeal to Congress to deregulate the banking, trucking, railroad, and communications industries and to lift the ceiling on returns for small savers, and tax measures to spur productivity once the budget is balanced and overall fiscal discipline is achieved.

These strong and decisive measures on both inflation and energy should carry the United States a substantial way toward meeting our major priorities of reducing inflation, adjusting to higher energy prices, reducing our vulnerability to OPEC price and supply decisions, and improving the efficiency and productivity of our economy. They should be most welcome to Saudi Arabia and, indeed, all countries which have a vital stake in the stability of both our own economy and that of the world as a whole.

**Commercial Ties**

The Saudis have also been using their oil revenues to import ever-increasing quantities of goods and services. Total Saudi imports have grown from

$2 billion in 1973 to around $24 billion in 1979. The United States has captured the largest share of the Saudi market in recent years, usually over 20 percent. United States exports to Saudi Arabia have increased dramatically, from $400 million in 1973 to $4.9 billion in 1979. Saudi Arabia has become the United States' seventh largest export market. In terms of two-way trade, Saudi Arabia is also our seventh largest trading partner.

Continued strong growth in U.S. exports to Saudi Arabia is anticipated in the future, despite active European and Asian competition. United States exports to Saudi Arabia reflect the technological superiority of U.S. products and U.S. responsiveness to Saudi needs. However, this favored position is dependent upon U.S. goods remaining cost competitive, since there are few areas in which alternatives to American technology are not available. In addition, Saudi Arabia is increasingly cost-conscious as it seeks to maximize the developmental impact of its oil earnings.

In addition to merchandise trade, United States business involvement in the Kingdom includes an estimated $1 billion in service transfers such as architectural, consulting, engineering and construction services which affect all phases of Saudi development programs. For example:

> U.S. companies prepared the master plans for major industrial complexes at Jubail and Yanbu and are managing construction of these projects.
>
> U.S. firms designed huge new airports at Jidda, Riyadh and Dhahran/Jubail and are managing construction at the first two.
>
> U.S. firms are involved in city planning at Jidda and Dammam, sewer construction in Jidda, and the transpeninsular crude oil pipeline from the oil fields to Yanbu.

Over 400 U.S. firms currently have offices in the Kingdom. Over 30,000 Americans are living in Saudi Arabia, as testimony to U.S. industry's involvement. We want to encourage and expand U.S.-Saudi commercial ties, with mutual benefits for both the United States and Saudi Arabia. The Saudis are particularly interested in using more small and medium-sized American firms as joint venture partners. This is an area on which your group may wish to focus.

The United States has taken a number of practical steps to expand its commercial ties with Saudi Arabia. In 1978, the President signed into law amendments to the Internal Revenue Code concerning the tax treatment of Americans working overseas. These amendments afford qualified U.S. taxpayers living in Saudi Arabia, as well as in other foreign countries, heretofore unavailable deductions for the costs associated with living overseas. An additional $5,000 deduction is allowed to Americans living in Saudi Arabia and other hardship posts. In addition, the amendments restored the $20,000 exclusion for construction personnel and others living in work camps in Saudi Arabia and other hardship posts. Although the definitions relating to work camps were somewhat restrictive when initially proposed, those definitions have been substantially liberalized so the American employees living in typical Saudi Arabian work camps will be able to claim the $20,000 deduction.

We hope the U.S. will maintain and, hopefully, expand its share of the Saudi market. A possible means of achieving this may be through more frequent dialogue between American and Arab businessmen perhaps using organizations such as this one. You and your colleagues may want to give some thought to ways of strengthening our commercial ties with the Arab world.

## The Joint Economic Commission

I would now like to discuss another important aspect of our overall relationship—the U.S.-Saudi Joint Economic Commission. This subject is particularly timely because the fifth annual meeting of the Commission will take place in Washington on April 1st and 2nd with Secretary of the Treasury G. William Miller and Saudi Finance Minister Abalkhail heading up the respective delegations.

The Commission has been in existence for almost six years. The traumatic events of the fall of 1973—the Yom Kippur War and the oil embargo—obviously did not create economic interdependence, but they did serve to highlight the fact of international interdependence. During the following year the United States established a series of joint commissions with Egypt, Jordan, Saudi Arabia, and others. These were conscious efforts to strengthen political and economic—primarily economic—ties with countries of the Middle East region. The Joint Statement issued by Crown Prince Fahd and former Secretary of State Kissinger in 1974 expressed the mutual desire of Saudi Arabia and the United States to work together to "promote programs of industrialization, trade, manpower training, agriculture, and science and technology." Since that time, the Joint Commission has become an active mechanism to bring together the expertise of various parts of the U.S. and Saudi Arabian governments and their respective private sectors to pursue Saudi development goals.

Structurally, the Joint Commission has a system of parallel direction in which Secretary of the Treasury Miller and Minister of Finance and National Economy Mohammed Abalkhail serve as cochairs and Dr. Mansoor Al Turki and I serve as coordinators. All U.S. project personnel have counterparts from Saudi government agencies.

In order to support and coordinate Joint Commission work on the U.S. side, the Treasury Department established an Office of Saudi Arabian Affairs in Washington, and later an office of the U.S. Representation to the Joint Commission in Riyadh.

Technical cooperation programs under the Joint Commission are provided by the United States to the Saudi Arabian government on a cost-reimbursable basis in accordance with a technical cooperation agreement initially signed early in 1975. During Secretary Miller's visit to Riyadh last November, this agreement was formally extended for another five-year period. Projects are financed by drawing against a Saudi Arabian Trust Account which is held by the U.S. Treasury Department. United States specialists work side-by-side with Saudi counterparts on a multiyear basis in the various ministries and agencies. More than 150 of these specialists are now in Saudi Arabia.

To date, agreement has been reached on twenty major projects which cover a broad range of economic activities and which have a total ultimate value in excess of $750 million. Projects are being carried out in areas as diverse as vocational training and highway transportation. They share a common goal: the expansion of the Saudi Government's capability to plan, guide, and monitor its development effort.

I would like to focus on three project areas which offer major developmental benefits to Saudi Arabia: an electrification plan, cooperation in solar power development, and the building of vocational training centers through the Kingdom.

## Powergrid Project

One of the most significant tasks we have been asked by the Saudis to undertake, under the auspices of the Joint Commission, is the development of an Electrification Plan for the Kingdom which will cover the next twenty-five years. Saudi hopes for establishing a strong, relatively diverse economic base hinge directly on their ability to provide electrical power in adequate amounts in a cost-effective manner. And, by making electricity available to every Saudi, regardless of his station or location, the government is able to demonstrate its interest and concern for the well being of the populace.

When Minister Ghazi Al-Gosaibi of the Ministry of Industry and Electricity approached the Joint Commission to undertake this project, he stated that his goal was to "bring electricity into every home in the Kingdom." The enormity of that task can be realized only when we recognize that there has been no similar effort—on such a scale—anywhere in the world before. Saudi Arabia is a country about a third the size of the United

States, and many of its people are sparsely settled in small villages and towns scattered over much of the countryside.

Through this plan, the Saudis are trying to do in twenty-five years what it took us to accomplish in this country in over seventy-five. The plan calls for a nearly fortyfold increase in the generating capacity of the Saudi power industry. Demand is increasing at a rate of about 25 percent a year, compared to an annual increase of about five percent in the United States since 1973. The capital cost for the new generating, transmission and distribution facilities over the life of the plan will be over $70 billion when figured with a 7 percent annual inflation rate. Such an incredible expenditure will provide the Saudis with an electrification system about equal to what we enjoy in this country today.

## SOLERAS

A second major program involves U.S.-Saudi cooperation for solar energy development. This unique agreement is a jointly funded program under the auspices of the Joint Commission. Over the next five years, both the United States and Saudi Arabia will provide $50 million to the $100 million program agreement.

The first projects will include the design and installation of the world's largest solar photovoltaic electrical system for two existing villages about 50 kilometers from Riyadh. The villages are not reached by the national power grid. Household appliances, street lighting, and agricultural water pumps, now serviced by diesel generators, will be powered by this solar energy system.

In time, this $12 million solar village project could serve as the prototype for rural electric development in Saudi Arabia and other developing countries. The United States, the leader in photovoltaic cell manufacturing, could rap major benefits through the marketing of this sophisticated new technology.

Other projects expected to be initiated under the Solar Agreement this year include an engineering test of a large sun-powered air conditioner mounted on a commercial building in the United States. We also are planning projects to study the socioeconomic effects of the solar system on the two villages and the establishment of solar insulation-measuring stations at several sites in Saudi Arabia. Discussion will begin soon also for the testing of solar air conditioners in Saudi Arabia and the design and construction in the United States of a solar desalination device.

This exciting, innovative area of cooperation under the Joint Commission directly involves the U.S. Department of Energy and the Saudi Arabian National Center for Science and Technology and the U.S. Treasury and the

Saudi Ministry of Finance. The Solar Energy Research Institute, which is the national center for solar development in the United States, serves as the secretariat and program manager for the Agreement.

The U.S.-Saudi Solar Agreement is a practical statement about the need to reach quickly into the future for clean, economic, renewable technologies to provide energy for future generations. It is also one more manifestation of close collaboration between the United States and Saudi Arabia.

Aside from making a very real contribution to the advancement of solar technology, the SOLERAS agreement testifies to the importance Saudi Arabia places on the development of alternative energy resources and on encouraging energy conservation in general. This solar energy program mates the world's largest exporter of petroleum with the world's largest importer of petroleum. While it would be overly sanguine for us to expect major technological breakthroughs under the U.S.-Saudi Solar Energy Program, we believe that this cooperative effort will contribute substantially to stimulating research and development and could result in long-term payoffs in developing solar-powered alternatives to petroleum. We are especially pleased that the solar energy program includes educational exchanges and training programs for U.S. and Saudi students.

**VOTRAKON**

Vocational training is the largest of the Joint Commission projects, both in terms of anticipated total costs and in terms of numbers of Americans who are living in Saudi Arabia and working on the project. A lack of skilled manpower is widely acknowledged as one of the major obstacles to smooth and rapid development of the Kingdom and the first Five Year Development Plan identified manpower development and training as one of the Kingdom's highest priority needs.

The VOTRAKON project is designed to increase both the number and skills of Saudi craftsmen through systematic strengthening of vocational-training curricula and construction of additional training facilities. Work is well underway in the areas of machine shop trades, automotive repair, welding, diesel engine repair, air conditioning repair and refrigeration, electricity, and plumbing. Saudi Arabians will be trained in developing and using instructional materials incorporating the most modern techniques and equipment. High priority is also being given to building an effective on-the-job training program throughout the Kingdom.

Saudi and U.S. project personnel are working together to strengthen the administration of training programs, to establish an instructor training institute and an instructional materials development center. Labor market analysts are continually gathering and analyzing statistical information to assist the Ministry of Labor and Social Affairs in planning and managing all these training activities.

To expand the capacity of the Ministry's vocational training system, the U.S. Department of Labor and the General Services Administration are heavily involved in the design and construction of the new Instructor Training Institute as well as ten new training facilities and housing for both students and instructors at fifteen existing training sites.

As part of the overall project effort, a competitive plan is being prepared to expand an existing effort in the United States for preparing Saudi administrators and instructors for their jobs in the new training system. It is estimated that over three hundred Saudi personnel may be trained here in the United States as part of this project.

## Conclusion

I have emphasized the significance of U.S. interests vis-à-vis Saudi Arabia in the areas of oil, finance, commerce, and bilateral cooperation characterized by the Joint Economic Commission. The Joint Commission symbolizes the close relationship between the United States and Saudi Arabia and has emerged in its own right as an important vehicle for bilateral technical cooperation. The Commission work does not by any means encompass all American involvement in Saudi development. In fact, the vast majority of trade is carried on outside the aegis of the Commission. As in any relationship, certain differences may occur from time to time—hopefully, without imposing serious strains on the totality of that relationship. Our overall dealings with Saudi Arabia have been, and should continue to be, characterized by mutual understanding and confidence.

It is clear that Saudi Arabia, as the world's largest exporter of oil, and the United States, as the largest producer of goods and services, have interests which extend beyond our bilateral relationship to include a mutual desire for a strong global economy and world peace. For our part, the United States will continue to work diligently toward this objective in all the areas I have mentioned.

# 13 The United States and Brazil: A Framework for Future Economic Relations

During the past few years Brazil and the United States have made a concerted effort to work together in resolving some difficult bilateral economic issues. I am happy to say that these mutual efforts have borne fruit. They not only resolved the major economic issues outstanding between our countries but have helped to strengthen overall ties between us as well. Just last week, Secretary of the Treasury G. William Miller and I had the pleasure of meeting with the Planning and Finance Ministers of Brazil to continue the process of close consultation which has produced these results.

As the world enters a new decade, our economic relations will continue to expand and will increasingly focus on the broader role of the United States and Brazil as partners in managing the international economic system. Here are some thoughts about possible future directions for the U.S.-Brazil economic relationship.

## Global Developments

The prospects for the world's economy as we enter a new decade are stark and sobering. The world economic outlook for both the immediate and longer term hinges on political developments in the Middle East and on oil market developments. Many of the major factors in the outlook are on the pessimistic side. The world as a whole could well see less growth, higher inflation, and more external financing problems in the period ahead.

In spite of a weak worldwide growth outlook, inflation rates are rising everywhere. Industrial countries could face double-digit inflation range rates during 1980. Less developed countries (LDCs) could see an inflation of 35-40 percent.

Large external imbalances are also likely. We expect the OPEC surplus to mushroom to something like $120 billion in 1980—nearly double 1979's surplus. This surplus must be matched by an equivalent deficit for oil importers as a group, the bulk of which will have to be financed by borrowing in world capital markets where OPEC countries are placing most of their surplus funds. We have confidence that the financial system can accommodate the current high levels of oil prices without being severely strained. But we must monitor the situation closely.

Originally presented on February 25, 1980, before the Brazil-U.S. Business Council in Washington, D.C.

A number of countries—both developing countries (DCs) and LDCs—will need to take adjustment action to reduce their deficits and restrain domestic inflation. The International Monetary Fund (IMF) has substantial resources to provide support for such adjustment action and will have even more when the latest quota increase becomes effective. It is important that countries initiate adjustment promptly and go to the IMF at an early stage when necessary.

**Brazilian Development**

From this overview of the world economic outlook, let me turn to a few observations on Brazil. Over the past two decades Brazil has rapidly emerged as a major world economic power. Its impressive growth and development has catapulted it into a position of leadership within the developing world. Brazil's rapid progress has been clearly demonstrated by a broad range of economic indicators:

Since 1970, Brazil's real GNP has multiplied fivefold (in current dollars) to more than $200 billion. This represents nearly 20 percent of total GNP of the non-OPEC developing nations. Brazil is the eighth largest free market economy in the world, ahead of many OECD countries on this measure.

Brazil's annual real GNP growth in the past decade averaged 9.2 percent compared with only 4.9 percent for all developing countries, and about 3.1 percent for the industrialized countries.

In 1980, Brazilian exports could reach nearly $20 billion, or one-quarter of the total from all Latin American countries. On a worldwide basis it ranks second only to the United States as an exporter of food products. At the same time, industrial products now represent over 50 percent of total Brazilian exports.

Brazil's excellent economic record and potential have enabled it to become one of the top five international borrowers in the world and the largest single foreign customer of the United States banks, which now have a total of nearly $15 billion in outstanding loans to Brazil.

It is also the largest single borrower from the World Bank and Inter-American Development Bank, which have lent Brazil a combined total of over $7.5 billion. Through these and other investments Brazil has now developed to the point where it has also begun to assist some of its less fortunate neighbors, as demonstrated by its contributions to the International Development Association and the African Development

> Fund, as well as by its initiatives in the Inter-American Development Bank (IDB) to make a larger proportion of its contribution to IDB resources available for less developed countries.
>
> Brazil now plays host to more than $15 billion in foreign direct investment and ranks seventh in the world as a host for U.S. direct investment, which now equals more than $4 billion.

Brazil's enormous progress is not accidental. The "Brazilian miracle" is the result of a sophisticated and prolonged effort to raise the country into industrialized status. Although the road has not always been smooth, Brazil has been uniquely successful in this endeavor. Even during periods of severe international economic difficulty, such as in 1974-1975, Brazil managed to keep its economy growing at a brisk pace. As a result, Brazil now has the third largest GNP in the Western Hemisphere and is clearly in the vanguard among middle-income countries.

### Common Interests

In the present global environment, characterized by profound and rapid economic change, it is increasingly important for nations like Brazil and the United States to recognize their common interests, strengthen their cooperation in managing bilateral concerns, and devise a forward-looking approach in dealing with international economic issues. Some of the critical challenges include promoting an open and growing world trade and payments system, fostering a positive environment for international investment, insuring continued availability of financial resources to LDCs, stimulating the development of alternative energy sources, controlling global inflationary pressures, stabilizing world commodity prices, and insuring adequate rates of growth of global production.

Perhaps the most vivid example of this mutual concern is energy. As major oil-importing nations, the United States and Brazil are now going through a painful transition phase. In 1973, Brazil's oil import bill of about $1 billion absorbed 14 percent of total export earnings; this year, the total cost of its petroleum imports is likely to approach $10 billion, or about half of its expected export revenues. Brazil is now the largest oil-importing country in the world outside of the OECD.

By comparison, U.S. oil imports also grew dramatically from $7.6 billion in 1973 to about $60 billion in 1979. Now, every 1 percent increase in the price of oil adds over $800 million to the annual import bill of the United States and over $100 million to the annual import bill of Brazil.

The United States and Brazil also face considerable challenges in dealing with growing domestic inflationary pressures, while insuring balanced growth. In 1979, inflation rates in both the United States and Brazil surpassed levels previously reached in either nation during the 1970s. In attempting to achieve greater price stability and establish better balance in the external sector, our countries face the unfortunate prospect of lower economic growth and the possibility of rising unemployment.

At the same time, both countries are confronted with the prospect of global recession and rising protectionist pressures which could adversely affect our trade flows. As large exporters we must continue to combat these trends if our economies are to grow in a stable and sustainable fashion. It is essential that we work closely together with other nations to maintain an open world trading system. Our governments worked closely together in developing the new Subsidy/Countervailing Duty Code; I anticipate that we will continue to work closely in managing future trade problems and implementing the agreements we have achieved.

Similarly, we share a strong interest in developments in the international capital markets. Brazil is one of the world's most prominent borrowers of private credit, as well as the largest client of both the World Bank and the Inter-American Development Bank. It is also a highly attractive market for foreign equity investment which now totals about $15 billion, the highest among all the developing countries in the world. The United States, on the other hand, as the world's largest financial market, has been a source of much of these funds, both directly through private bank credits and U.S. business investment as well as indirectly through the multilateral development institutions to which the United States is the principal contributor.

Our countries both have an important stake in world commodity trade. Together we account for a significant share of trade in coffee, cocoa, soybeans, wheat, and bauxite. Consequently, instability in world markets has a large impact on the U.S. and Brazilian economies. By the same token, policy decisions by either country can have a large impact on world commodity markets. In view of our interest in stable markets, we could both benefit from regular discussions of commodity problems.

## Conclusions

We believe that an effective economic relationship between the United States and Brazil must continue to be based on the twin principles of shared responsibility and increased participation in international economic decisions.

The United States recognizes and supports an enhanced role for Brazil in the international economic system. At the same time, Brazil is considering how it can most effectively translate its enhanced position into both a greater role in the world economy and to insure maximum possible benefits for its own economic development. We believe that these dual goals are mutually consistent. While recognizing that Brazil still must overcome many of the pressing problems facing the developing world, such as widespread poverty and uneven income distribution, it can at the same time actively participate in the resolution of global economic issues. The challenge for the future economic relationship between the United States and Brazil is to strengthen and diversify the fundamental basis of our collaboration to deal with the complete spectrum of international economic problems which we both face, from our different perspectives but with underlying national interests which are very similar.

Brazil has recently undertaken fundamental adjustments in the management of its economy, which provide a firm foundation for such future collaboration and which mark a clear departure from the past. The policy reform measures announced by the government in December 1979 and further articulated since then demonstrate Brazil's determination to take comprehensive steps in order to achieve greater price stability and external adjustment. This set of reform measures included a significant liberalization of Brazil's foreign trade regime. The Brazilian government's action to eliminate immediately its principal export subsidies, raise interest rates gradually on subsidized export credits, cancel the prior import deposit requirements, and revise the Law of Similars further demonstrates its strong commitment to an open world trading system. As a result of these and other actions, a source of earlier trade frictions with the United States and other countries has been finally eliminated.

Brazil has also stepped up its efforts to adjust to the global scarcity of energy resources and reduce its growing dependence on imported petroleum, thereby contributing as well to the global energy balance. Perhaps most notable is its ambitious program to free its 6.5 million vehicles from gasoline and run them on alcohol. The government has already spent $2.5 billion on this effort and is budgeting almost twice that amount for the next five years.

Reconciling Brazil's desire for continued rapid expansion of the domestic economy with the need to establish better balance in the external sector has not been an easy task. The recent policy measures adopted by the government should enhance the confidence of foreign investors and lending institutions in the soundness of Brazil's development prospects. Moreover, the successful implementation of these policies should significantly contribute to the continued dynamism of the Brazilian economy and to its ultimate emergence as a full-fledged industrial power. While we recognize that Brazil cannot achieve this overnight, the demonstrated resilience of the Brazilian economy to internal and external difficulties suggests that with continued perserverance it can readily adjust to new global realities.

There are many areas where the prospects for further collaboration, based on policies already undertaken in both the United States and Brazil, are bright:

> In the trade field, most bilateral problems are now behind us. As Brazil continues to reap greater benefits from world trade, we encourage it to continue to liberalize its trade policies.
>
> Increased interdependence will elevate the need for closer and more active consultations about trends in the world economy. Our discussions with the Brazilian Finance and Planning ministers represent part of an ongoing process to exchange views on important economic and financial issues. We expect that this process will continue to grow in the future.
>
> We believe the possibilities for cooperation in the investment field are also worthy of increased attention. The scope is broad, including issues such as the transfer of technology, taxation of royalties and profits from foreign investment, and the role of official investment incentives and performance requirements. We should together work toward agreement on a common basis for new "rules of the game" for international investment.
>
> Given our respective positions as major agricultural exporters, the United States and Brazil have a common ground from which to pursue closer cooperation on commodities trade.
>
> We should also seek closer cooperation in devising innovative solutions to our respective energy needs. While a bilateral framework already exists in this area, we should step up our technology exchanges in the development of alternative sources of energy.

These are only a few of the areas where we can develop a common foundation for further, even closer partnership between the United States and Brazil. I could mention many others such as technology transfer, strengthening the international financial institutions, and so forth. But the pattern should now be clear. Together we can and should serve as constructive forces for remolding the world to accommodate new interests and new realities. Only by such close cooperation can we hope to achieve a peaceful, prosperous, and successful global economic system.

# 14 The United States and Mexico in the World Economy

Last year I had the pleasure of addressing members of the U.S.-Mexico Chamber of Commerce in Washington and again in Mexico regarding U.S.-Mexican trade relations and Mexico's emerging role in the global economy. I emphasized the importance of Mexican participation in the international economic system and the potential benefits of Mexican accession to the GATT (general agreement on tariffs and trades) and signature of the new Code on Subsidies and Countervailing Measures. Since then, Mexico's role in the world economy has expanded and Mexico has taken an important decision with regard to its future trade relations.

## Mexico and International Finance

Mexico has recognized the key role it can play in the management of the international economy through new initiatives in the areas of development assistance and international finance. The United States welcomes these important contributions, which are consistent with Mexico's growing economic stature.

As a charter member of the World Bank and the Inter-American Development Bank (IDB), Mexico has benefited from a total of more than $5 billion in loans from these institutions and has been the second largest borrower from them. In recognition of its relatively advanced standing among developing nations of the hemisphere, Mexico has now begun to assist its poorer neighbors through these institutions while continuing to help finance its own development under their credit facilities. In particular:

> Mexico has agreed to contribute for the first time to the International Development Association (IDA), the window of the World Bank which provides long-term concessional loans to the poorest developing countries. In doing so, Mexico joins Brazil, Argentina, and Venezuela as Latin American Contributors to IDA.
>
> Mexico, Argentina, and Brazil have agreed to limit their joint borrowing from the IDB to $750 million per year during the period 1979-1982,

Originally presented on July 9, 1980, before the United States-Mexican Chamber of Commerce in Washington, D.C.

the same as their average annual borrowing during 1976-1978. At this constant level, their annual borrowing in real terms will decline, leaving a greater share of the rising level of Bank lending for the poorer countries of the region.

Mexico has agreed not to borrow hard currency from the IDB's concessional window, the Fund for Special Operations, and has tripled the hard currency portion of its contributions to that window from 25 percent to 75 percent.

Together, these measures will help ensure that a larger proportion of IDB resources, and additional IDA resources, will be available to the needier developing countries, especially within the hemisphere. In view of Mexico's improved current account prospects because of growing petroleum exports receipts, a relative reduction in its extensive borrowing from the international financial institutions seems appropriate. This evolving role would also seem to make good sense in terms of Mexico's own economic and political interests in the hemisphere, especially in Central America and the Caribbean.

Also in the area of international finance, a Task Force on Non-Concessional Financial Flows proposed and chaired by Mexico has been created under the auspices of the IMF/World Bank Development Committee. The Task Force is assessing prospective nonconcessional flows to developing countries over the next few years and reviewing proposals to assure an adequate level of such flows. Its work, which we strongly support, is especially timely in view of current concerns about the impact of oil price increases on the global financial system.

Unfortunately, at the same time that Mexico is moving to the forefront in international financial affairs, it has taken a major step backward in deciding not to join the GATT. This is most unfortunate. Mexico's responsibility and interest in international trade is just as great, and just as important, as its participation in international financial matters. Its decision has significant implications for the future development of Mexican trade, both in relation to the United States and within the international trading system as a whole. I would like to explore some of the implications of this step and pose some questions about where we go from here.

## Mexico and the World Trading System

Mexico is now embarked on an ambitious new development program which seeks to utilize its new-found oil wealth to spur rapid economic growth. We have strongly supported the objectives of the Mexican development plan, which seek inter alia increased employment, more equitable distribution of income, growth and decentralization of industrial production, and an expansion of trade.

Mexico's economic planners have obviously been torn between the desire to conserve national resources to promote stable, noninflationary growth and the need to increase exports to pay for essential capital goods imports and foodstuffs. On the one hand, there is the desire not to rely excessively on oil exports and to limit oil production to levels that will foster stable domestic growth. On the other hand, Mexico needs to export to pay for essential capital goods imports, to help diversify its industrial base, and to market production generated from new plants which the Mexican economy cannot now absorb.

Both of these objectives are important; both require greater Mexican participation in world trade. It is therefore, particularly unfortunate that Mexico has decided not to join the GATT at this time. Only a few major developing countries are not members of the GATT. This decision isolates Mexico from the principal world trade forum at a time when the very rules that Mexican negotiators worked so hard to revise, to accommodate the needs of developing countries, are being put into place for trade among GATT signatories.

Mexico has not only given up these important benefits, in deciding not to join GATT, it has also turned down the very generous terms negotiated in its protocol of accession. This agreement in effect enabled Mexico to pursue its development programs and to continue to protect its domestic industries and agricultural sector for the next ten to twelve years.

The Mexican protocol was by far the most flexible granted to a country acceding to the GATT, as the result of a negotiation in which the United States went to great lengths to meet all the concerns of the Mexican government. That protocol is now null and void. President Lopez-Portillo recognized in his speech on March 18 that he did not expect that Mexico would ever be offered such good terms in the future.

In addition, Mexico has sacrificed concessions negotiated in many bilateral tariff agreements. The U.S.-Mexican MTN agreement contained tariff cuts by the U.S. on \$232 million of industrial and \$304 million of agricultural exports from Mexico. In exchange, Mexico had offered tariff concessions on only \$153 million of industrial and \$159 million of agricultural exports from the United States. Our concessions on industrial products were to have covered numerous products which are highly import-sensitive such as textile and apparel items, ceramic tiles, and glassware. Over half of our agricultural concessions covered imports of fruit and vegetable products of particular interest to Mexico.

During the past year, I spoke to your group about the specific benefits which would flow from Mexican participation in the GATT. These benefits derive from one simple fact: Mexico recognizes that it needs to greatly increase its exports to spur domestic growth, and GATT membership offers the best safeguard that Mexican exports will be afforded liberal access to foreign markets. That conclusion remains valid today.

Instead of dwelling on lost opportunities, however important, we need to examine what happens next and how it will affect U.S.-Mexican trade relations. For example, there has been a great deal of speculation that Mexico might seek a bilateral agreement with the United States to gain concessions arising from the MTN agreements covering most of its trade. I am not sanguine, however, that such a comprehensive trade agreement could be worked out.

First of all, the most important concessions made by the United States in the MTN involve reciprocal rights and obligations under the various nontariff measures codes, especially the Code on Subsidies and Countervailing Measures (to which I will refer in more detail in just a moment). To benefit from these concessions, a country must be a signatory to each particular code—though not necessarily to the GATT itself. Thus in particular, Mexico would not be eligible for an injury test under the U.S. countervailing duty (CVD) law until it signed the Subsidies Code, or assumed essentially the same Code obligations with respect to the United States. Likewise, Mexico would be barred from the opportunity to bid on U.S. government contracts that are covered by the new Government Procurement Code. Mexico's lack of participation in Geneva effectively removes most major NTB problems from future bilateral negotiations.

U.S. law ties Code benefits to Code participation. The United States and other MTN participants are dedicated to making the Codes important instruments in conducting trade and managing trade disputes. Therefore, we will make every effort to preserve the integrity of these agreements.

Obviously, one important variable has been left out of the above equation: oil. Some have argued that Mexico should negotiate a series of bilateral agreements, using oil exports as leverage to obtain trade concessions for other Mexican exports.

Clearly, Mexico's trade relations with the major trading nations have to be expanded to accommodate the export objectives of the new development plan. As already noted, the United States fully supports these Mexican objectives. But Mexico's trade prospects would seem to depend primarily on its ability to produce goods that other countries want to buy and the economic strength, and hence, demand of those countries for imported goods. We certainly welcome increased Mexican oil exports as an important new source of supply helpful in dampening pressures for new oil price increases, but history reveals no case of any country's successfully bartering access to its oil (or other) exports for bilateral trade concessions from a diverse group of importing countries.

In the end, the simple fact remains that almost 70 percent of Mexico's trade is with the United States. Good U.S.-Mexican trade relations are essential for the success of the Mexican development plan. Absent GATT membership, with its built-in rights and safeguards for access to foreign markets, we need to be particularly sensitive to protectionist pressures that could lead to a contraction rather than a growth in this bilateral trade.

There is, in fact, growing concern in the United States that Mexico wants all the benefits of international cooperation without assuming any of the responsibilities thereof. This attitude reflects in part our disappointment over Mexico's failure to join GATT, but it also reflects unhappiness over Mexican trade policies that both restrict U.S. exports and lure U.S. investments across the border. This is particularly troublesome for the U.S. auto industry which is moving south (and north) of the border in response to lucrative investment incentives. Because these grants are contingent on local content and export performance requirements, they encourage sales back to the U.S. market, exacerbating unemployment in an already hard-pressed industry—and political pressures for countermeasures. The use of such incentives by Mexico and other nations has already generated proposals in the U.S. Congress for the imposition of value-added requirements for all autos sold in the United States.

In addition, there are serious potential problems in the not so distant future as more and more Mexican firms begin to take advantage of the vast array of export incentives offered under the new development plan. As I have noted already, because Mexico has not signed the Subsidies Code and thus is not afforded an injury test under the U.S. countervailing duty law, any export that benefits from Mexico's development subsidies could be liable to an automatic added duty. The U.S. government is obligated to process all CVD complaints thoroughly and expeditiously. Since subsidies are such an integral part of the development plan, this could become a pervasive problem for U.S.-Mexico trade relations.

The United States does not wish to erect new barriers to trade. Indeed, our record is very good in resisting pressures to do so—and, in fact, in liberalizing trade further through the MTN, GSP, and other measures. Unless Mexico plays its part, however, we may be constrained by our own law to bar the very products that are an essential part of the Mexican development programs which we all want to succeed.

## Conclusion

Mexico has played an innovative, leadership role in the international financial arena. As Mexico's impressive development continues, it is clearer than ever that its future lies in expanding its ties to the international trading system as well.

This relationship is bound to develop as a matter of course, needing no push from the United States or any of Mexico's other trading partners. Over time, it seems inevitable that Mexico will become a de facto—and probably de jure—member of the GATT system.

This process will proceed at a pace chosen by Mexico, however. The United States should not react with threats of any kind, nor will we do so. Each country benefits too much from the existing trade relationship to allow the disappointment over the GATT decision to color its attitude on bilateral trade matters.

But it must be recognized, on both sides of the border, that the United States cannot extend the same trade benefits to countries which do not adhere to GATT agreements as it does to GATT members and that it will be obliged to enforce its own laws concerning unfair trade practices. Those who share the benefits of trade must also share responsibility for the management of the world trading system. Mexico has already accepted this premise on the financial side; we hope it will move forward on trade as well.

# Index

# Index

## About the Author

**C. Fred Bergsten** is a Senior Associate at the Carnegie Endowment for International Peace. He served as Assistant Secretary for International Affairs at the Treasury Department from 1977 until January 1981. He was a Senior Fellow of the Brookings Institution from 1972 through 1976. From January 1968 until May 1971, he was Assistant for International Economic Affairs to the Assistant to the President for National Security Affairs. From 1963 to 1967 he was in the Office of International Monetary Affairs at the Department of State.

Dr. Bergsten has published several books and numerous articles on a wide range of international economic issues. He received the master's and Ph.D. degrees from the Fletcher School of Law and Diplomacy. Dr. Bergsten is listed in *Who's Who in America* and was cited as one of "200 Young American Leaders" by *Time* in 1974.

Reassuring

Oil

Co-op^n

Int'l Banks as channels